The Book of Isaiah

Christ, Our Redeemer

Lucian Farrar, Jr.

James Kay Publishing

Tulsa, Oklahoma

Christ, Our Redeemer
The Book of Isaiah
ISBN 978-1-943245-29-1

www.jameskaypublishing.com

e-mail: sales@jameskaypublishing.com

© 2018 Lucian Farrar, Jr.

Cover design by JKP
Author Photo by Bob Cooper

1.4
All rights reserved.
No part of this book may be reproduced in any form or by any means
— except for review questions or brief quotations —
without permission in writing from the author.

also by
Lucian Farrar, Jr.

The Victorious Church
In the Book of Revelation
A Commentary and Questions

The Book of Daniel
The Most High Rules
A Commentary and Questions

The Life of Christ

The Minor Prophets
God's Spokesmen
A Commentary and Questions

Psalms – Book 1
David's Original Collection

Scriptures are from the King James Version
with archaic words, forms, and punctuations
replaced by those in current use.

Other translations are acknowledged
by the following abbreviations:

ASV – American Standard Version
ESV – English Standard Version
NASB – New American Standard Bible, 1973 Edition
NIV – New International Version, 1996 Edition
NKJV – New King James Version

Dedication

This book is dedicated to Ralph Hunter, who stirred my interest in The Book of Isaiah by a course that he taught at the Owasso School of Biblical Studies. Ralph began preaching in 1959. He has served as a minister of the gospel in Temple, Texas and the Oklahoma cities of Kingfisher, Stigler, Idabel, and Collinsville. While at Idabel, he went on a three-month mission trip in India. Ralph served five years as a missionary in New Castle, Australia, from 1972 to 1977. Ralph has written a book, *Life Without...*, relating experiences during his jail/prison ministry of 32 years. Ralph Hunter has touched many lives for good in God's service.

— Lucian Farrar, Jr.

Table of Contents

Dedication ix

Isaiah, The Messianic Prophet 1

Isaiah 1 - 5, Charges Against Jerusalem 9

Isaiah 6 - 9, The Coming of Immanuel 23

Isaiah 10 - 12, The Peaceful Kingdom 35

Isaiah 13 - 20, God Judges the Nations 45

Isaiah 21 - 27, God Punishes the Nations 55

Isaiah 28 - 35, Woes and Blessings 73

Isaiah 36 - 39, Hezekiah's Prayers Answered 91

Isaiah 40 - 43, The Lord Brings Comfort 107

Isaiah 44 - 48, The Lord, Your Redeemer 121

Isaiah 49 - 53, The Suffering Servant 137

Isaiah 54 - 57, The Covenant of Peace 157

Isaiah 58 - 66, The Glorious Future 173

The Messianic Prophet

*"Though your sins are as scarlet,
they shall be as white as snow."*
Isaiah 1:18

Isaiah is called "The Messianic Prophet" because of his many descriptive prophecies concerning Christ, our Redeemer, including his virgin birth, his death for our sins, his burial, and his resurrection. Isaiah revealed the gospel of Christ in advance. (1 Corinthians 15:1-4)

The Book of Isaiah is the first of the Major Prophets. It is like a miniature Bible with its sixty-six chapters. The first thirty-nine chapters are like the thirty-nine books of the Old Testament with judgments upon sinful men. But the last twenty-seven chapters have a message of hope corresponding to the twenty-seven books of the New Testament. Isaiah's people would be punished for their sins, but repentance would bring forgiveness. The prophet predicted not only the destruction of Jerusalem and the temple but also their restoration. Isaiah had a message of hope for his nation and for the world. The theme of the book is in Isaiah 1:18, "Though your sins are as scarlet, they shall be white as snow."

Isaiah – the Man

His name means "the LORD saves." He prophesied **in the days of Uzziah, Jotham, Ahaz, and Hezekiah, kings of Judah. 1:1** According to the Jewish Talmud, Isaiah and king Uzziah were first cousins. Isaiah's father Amoz was a brother of Amaziah, the father of king Uzziah. (2 Chronicles 26:1) Isaiah was married to a prophetess (8:3), and they had at least two sons: Shear-jashub (7:3) and Maher-shalal-hash-baz (8:3). His call to be a prophet was in the year that Uzziah died. (6:1-8)

Amos and Hosea prophesied in the northern kingdom of Israel, a short time before Isaiah and the prophet Micah spoke to the southern kingdom of Judah. Isaiah lived in Jerusalem and was an advisor to the kings of Judah. He is often called "The Prince of the Prophets."

Date & Setting

The book of Isaiah was written about 740 to 680 BC. By the middle of the eighth century BC, Israel and Judah had restored their borders and enjoyed a prosperity that was equal to the time of Solomon. But the two nations had forgotten God and had fallen into immorality and political corruption. Both kingdoms would be punished for forsaking the LORD. During the time of King Ahaz, Judah was threatened first by Syria and the northern kingdom of Israel. Assyria became a great power when Tiglath-Pileser III took the throne in 745 BC. [1] His army defeated all their enemies, and an annual tribute payment was exacted from countries as proof of their loyalty. If they rebelled, their cities were besieged until they surrendered. Their people were either killed or deported to other parts of the Assyrian Empire. These policies were continued by his successors, Shalmaneser, Sargon II, and Sennacherib. The northern kingdom of Israel fell when Samaria, its capital city, was destroyed in 722 BC after Shalmaneser besieged it for three years. The powerful Assyrian army also destroyed forty fortified cities of Judah, and Sennacherib surrounded the city of Jerusalem. Isaiah and King Hezekiah of Judah were in the city during this siege. But due to their faith in God, Jerusalem was spared. (Isaiah 36 - 37)

---

[1] Tiglath-Pileser III is called "Pul" in 2 Kings 15:19 and 1 Chronicles 5:2

The Unity of Isaiah

Until the late eighteenth century, all sixty-six chapters of the Book of Isaiah were recognized as the writings of one person: the prophet Isaiah. The Jewish Talmud, the Septuagint Greek translation of the Old Testament, and the first century Jewish historian Josephus all attribute the book to Isaiah. Liberal critics insist that the book was written by two or more writers over a long period of time. Some critics refer to chapters 40-66 as "Deutero-Isaiah" (or second Isaiah) because of the change in style of writing and in the theology. These critics forget that the writer's purpose will dictate these changes. Isaiah is showing God's judgments upon sinners in chapters 1-39 and the hope and comfort that will be in God's Servant, the Messiah, in chapters 40-66.

These critics also make the statement that the prophets always used the future tense to predict future events. Based on this false assumption, they seek to prove that chapters 40-66 were written after the Babylonian exile. They quote Isaiah 40:1-2 and Isaiah 45:1. The messianic prophecy of Isaiah 53 is also in this section. The New Testament declares that Isaiah 53 is about the Christ in Acts 8:30-35 and in 1 Peter 2:21-24. This prophecy is in the past tense. Isaiah 53:4 says, "Surely, he **has borne** our griefs and **carried** our sorrows." This proves the premise of the critics is false. God's prophetic promises are so certain that they may be stated in the past tense. This is seen in the promises made to Abraham. Romans 4:17 says, "As it is written, 'I **have made** you a father of many nations.'" This promise was made in Genesis 17:5, when God changed his name from Abram to Abraham, even before Isaac was born. Paul then writes of "God, who gives life to the dead and **calls those things which do not exist as though they did.**" NKJV

Isaiah describes God as **"The Holy One of Israel."** This description occurs twenty-five times in the book: twelve times in chapters 1–39, thirteen times in chapters 40–66. This description appears only six times elsewhere in the Bible. Hailey concludes, "In none of the twenty-one passages in the New Testament where the writer or speaker quotes Isaiah and appeals to the prophet by name is there any hint of suspicion that more than one Isaiah wrote the book bearing that title." [2]

The Great Isaiah Scroll of the Dead Sea Scrolls was written over one hundred years before the birth of Christ. This proves that the amazing predictions by Isaiah concerning Christ our Redeemer are true prophecy.[3]

An Outline of the Book of Isaiah

I. Prophecies of Condemnation (Chapters 1 - 39)
II. Prophecies of Comfort (Chapters 40 - 66)

The Kings during the Time of Isaiah's Prophecies

Israel	Assyria	Judah
Jeroboam II (782-753 BC)	Shalmaneser IV (783-755 BC)	Uzziah (Azariah) (767-739 BC)
	Ashur-dan III (773-755)	
Zechariah (753-752)	Ashur-nirari V (755-745)	
Shallum (752)		
Menahem (752-742)	Tiglath-Pileser III (Pul) (745-727)	Jotham (739-732)
Pekahiah (742-740)		Ahaz (732-715)
Pekah (740-732)		
Hoshea (732-722)	Shalmaneser V (727-722)	
	Sargon (722-705)	Hezekiah (715-686)
	Sennacherib (705-681)	

---

[2] Homer Hailey, *Commentary on Isaiah,* p. 29
[3] Neil R. Lightfoot, *How We Got the Bible,* p. 136

Review Questions on Isaiah

1. Isaiah is called "The _____ Prophet."

2. What is the theme of Isaiah in Isaiah 1:18?
   _____
   _____

3. The book of Isaiah is called "a miniature Bible." Why?
   _____
   _____
   _____

4. The name "Isaiah" means _____ _____ _____.

5. Isaiah prophesied during the reigns of what four kings?
   _____

6. Isaiah was married to a _____.

7. Isaiah and _____ were speaking to the kingdom of Judah shortly after _____ and _____ were prophets in the northern kingdom of Israel.

8. Isaiah lived in the city of _____ and was an advisor to the _____ of Judah.

9. Because he was related to the kings of Judah, Isaiah is called "The _____ of the Prophets."

10. The book was written about _____ to _____ BC.

11. During Isaiah's time, the kingdom of Judah at first was threatened by _____ and _____ and later by _____

12. The northern kingdom of Israel fell when Samaria, its capital city, was destroyed in _____ BC.

13. What three ancient authorities testify that Isaiah was written by one man, the prophet Isaiah?
    _____
    _____
    _____

14. God uses _____ tense to predict future events. Romans 4:17 says God "calls those things which do not _____ as though they _____." ᴺᴷᴶⱽ

15. God is described twenty-five times in the book of Isaiah as "the _____ _____ of Israel."
    _____ times in chapters 1-39
    _____ times in chapters 40-66.

16. The Outline of Isaiah:
    I. Chapters 1-39, _____
    II. Chapters 40-66, _____

Part I

Prophecies of Condemnation

Isaiah 1 – 39

Charges Against Jerusalem
Isaiah 1 – 5

The vision of Isaiah the son of Amoz, which he saw concerning Judah and Jerusalem in the days of Uzziah, Jotham, Ahaz and Hezekiah, kings of Judah. 1:1 The book of Isaiah is called **the vision of Isaiah.** We read in 2 Chronicles 32:32, "Now the rest of the acts of Hezekiah, and his goodness, behold, they are written in **the vision of Isaiah**." Prophecies about other nations were revealed to Isaiah by the LORD, because they concerned Judah. Liberal critics say the book is the work of an editor, because Isaiah refers to himself in the third person, "he", in Isaiah 1:1, 2:1, 13:1, and 20:2. The book is a collection of several messages of the prophet, but Isaiah himself is the editor who arranged his book in its present order. Isaiah wrote these words to give the setting for his writings; they do not indicate another writer or editor as liberal critics insist. Hailey refers to this verse as "Isaiah's Personal Introduction to His Book." [4]

God Brings Charges Against His People
Isaiah 1:2-15

Hear, O heavens, and give ear, O earth, for the LORD has spoken. "I have nourished and brought up children, and they have rebelled against me." 1:2 As a lawyer in a court of law, Isaiah calls upon the heavens and earth to witness the charges that God brings against his people. The LORD's complaint is that his children have rebelled against him.

---

[4] Homer Hailey, *Commentary on Isaiah*, p. 35

"The ox knows his owner, and the donkey his master's crib; but Israel does not know, my people do not consider." 1:3 Even animals know their master, the one that provides for them, but God's people do not recognize him as the source of their blessings. **Israel** is referring to both the kingdom of Judah and the kingdom of Israel. The LORD had blessed united Israel, by bringing their nation out of bondage into the land of promise, but they were guilty of rebelling against him.

Isaiah describes the sinful nation as being **a people laden with iniquity, a seed of evildoers, children that are corrupters. They have forsaken the LORD. They have provoked the Holy One of Israel unto anger; they have gone away backward. 1:4** The condition of the nation is figuratively described as a person whose **head is sick and the whole heart is faint. From the sole of the foot even unto the head there is no soundness in it, but wounds and bruises and putrefying sores; they have not been closed up, neither bound up, neither mollified with ointment. 1:5-6** In the future, they would literally suffer these things, when conquered by their enemies.

Your country is desolate. Your cities are burned with fire ... So, the daughter of Zion is left ... as a hut in a garden of cucumbers, as a besieged city. Unless the LORD of hosts had left us a very small remnant, we would have become like Sodom; we would have been made like Gomorrah. 1:7-9 ᴺᴷᴶⱽ Isaiah speaks of the destruction that would soon come to the kingdom of Judah. After the fall of Israel, cities of Judah also would be conquered, and Jerusalem, the daughter of Zion, would be besieged. Only a **remnant** would be left. Their only hope would be deliverance by the LORD. This prophecy is fulfilled in Isaiah 36-37 and in 2 Kings 18-19.

The LORD asks, **"To what purpose is the multitude of your sacrifices to me?" 1:10-11** Their rulers were like Sodom and their people were like Gomorrah. Sacrifices, assemblies, and festivals were commanded in the Law of Moses, but the people were not honoring God with their lives. The LORD had enough of their insincere worship. God did not delight in their assemblies and sacrifices. Because of their sins, he would not hear them when they spread their hands in prayer. **1:12-15**

The Call for Repentance and Forgiveness
Isaiah 1:16-20

"Wash you, make you clean. Put away the evil of your doings from before my eyes. Cease to do evil; learn to do well." 1:16-17 They were to seek justice, relieve the oppressed, help the fatherless and widows.

"Come now, and let us reason together," says the LORD. "Though your sins are as scarlet, they shall be as white as snow." 1:18 Don Shackelford gives the following explanation: "God offers salvation to all, but it must be accepted on His terms. In the Christian Age, this means that we must hear the gospel, believe it, repent of our sins, and be baptized into Christ (Rom. 10:13-17; Acts 2:38)." [5]

"If you are willing and obedient, you shall eat the good of the land. But if you refuse and rebel, you shall be devoured by the sword." 1:19-20 Their decision would determine their destiny. The same is true today. Our choices determine our future.

---

[5] Don Shackelford, *Truth for Today Commentary--Isaiah*, p. 39

How has the faithful city become a harlot! 1:21 Jerusalem once was faithful to God, but it had become unfaithful. The city once was full of righteousness and justice, but now was full of murderers and thieves. Their princes were rebellious, and they loved to take bribes as they refused to defend the fatherless and widows. **1:22-23**

Therefore the LORD of hosts declares, **"I will get relief from my foes and avenge myself on my enemies, I will turn my hand against you; I will thoroughly purge away your dross and remove your impurities." 1:24-25** ^{NIV} The foes and enemies of the LORD were the unfaithful inhabitants of Jerusalem. God is predicting the destruction of the city in 586 BC. However, he promises, **"I will restore your judges as at the first, your counselors as at the beginning; afterward you shall be called, the city of righteousness, the faithful city. Zion shall be redeemed with justice and her converts with righteousness." 1:26-27** Jerusalem would be rebuilt. God would redeem the city after punishing it. God's spiritual kingdom, the church, would be established there. (2:2-4) The church is called the New Jerusalem, the holy city, in Revelation 21:2-10. This New Jerusalem is "the city of righteousness, the faithful city."

And they that forsake the LORD shall be consumed. 1:28 The unfaithful were consumed by the destructions of Jerusalem both in 586 BC and in AD 70. All who forsake the Lord will suffer "everlasting destruction from the presence of the Lord and from the glory of his power," according to 2 Thessalonians 1:7-9 and Revelation 21:8.

When God's judgment comes, the unfaithful will be ashamed of those things that caused them to forsake the LORD. **1:29-31**

The Future Kingdom of God
Isaiah 2:1-5

The word that Isaiah the son of Amoz saw concerning Judah and Jerusalem, 2:1 This introduces a new message from God to Isaiah. Earthly Jerusalem would be destroyed in AD 70, but before its destruction, a spiritual heavenly Jerusalem would come out of Zion. It would be the eternal kingdom of the LORD's house.

And it shall come to pass in the last days, that the mountain of the LORD's house shall be established in the top of the mountains and shall be exalted above the hills; and all nations shall flow unto it. 2:2 "The last days" refer to the Christian Age, when the house of God is "the church of the living God." (1 Timothy 3:15) In prophecy, a **mountain** is a symbol for a kingdom. The kingdom of Babylon is called a "destroying mountain" in Jeremiah 51:25. In Daniel 2:28-44, the stone that struck the great statue representing four kingdoms became a great mountain that filled the whole earth. Daniel interpreted this "mountain" to be the eternal kingdom that God would establish in the days of the Roman Empire. (Daniel 2:44). Daniel said he was making known what would be "**in the latter days**." (Daniel 2:28) The stone that was "cut out without hands" is the confession that "Jesus is the Christ the Son of the living God" revealed by God the Father. Jesus said upon this rock, he would build his church kingdom. (Matthew 16:16-19) Therefore, the mountain of the LORD's house refers to the kingdom of God, the church of Christ.

Jesus said that the kingdom of God would come with power (Mark 9:1) and that the apostles would receive this power when the Holy Spirit came upon them. (Acts 1:1-8) Jesus instructed his apostles to remain in Jerusalem until they were given power from on high. (Luke 24:29) This prophecy was fulfilled on Pentecost. (Acts 2:1-4) On that day, Peter quoted the prophet Joel, **"And it shall come to pass in the last days,"** says God, "I will pour out of my Spirit." (Acts. 2:16-21) Joel began his prophecy with the same words that are in Isaiah 2:2, **"And it shall come to pass in the last days."** Peter then used Psalm 16:8-11 to prove that Christ would be raised from the dead to sit on David's throne. (Acts 2:25-30) Peter then concluded, "Therefore let all the house of Israel know assuredly, that God has made that same Jesus, whom you have crucified, both Lord and Christ." (Acts 2:25-36)

And many people shall go and say, "Come, and let us go up to the mountain of the LORD**, to the house of the God of Jacob; and he will teach us of his ways, and we will walk in his paths, for out of Zion shall go forth the law, and the word of the L**ORD **from Jerusalem." 2:3** There were "devout men out of every nation" in Jerusalem on Pentecost, and they came together to hear the apostles, who were "filled with the Holy Spirit." (Acts 1:26 – Acts 2:12) Jesus had said "that repentance and remission of sins should be preached in his name among all nations, beginning at Jerusalem." (Luke 24:47) When Peter told believers to "repent and be baptized every one of you in the name of Jesus Christ for the remission of sins" (Acts 2:38), they that gladly received his word were baptized, and the same day there were added unto them about three thousand souls. (Acts 2:41) The prophecy of Isaiah 2:2-4 was fulfilled on the Day of Pentecost following Christ's resurrection. This church kingdom is the New Jerusalem, "the city of righteousness, the faithful city." (Isaiah 1:26) The gospel of Christ is preached to all the nations by the church. (Matthew 28:19-20; Mark 16:15-16)

And they shall beat their swords into plowshares, and their spears into pruninghooks; nation shall not

lift up sword against nation, neither shall they learn war anymore. 2:4 There is peace among all nations within Christ's church kingdom. (Ephesians 2:14-17) Unlike other religions that advance their beliefs with the sword, the disciples of Christ are to beat their swords into useful tools of peace. Former enemies become friends when they are converted to Jesus and his teachings.

The prophecies of Isaiah 2:2-4 and Micah 4:1-3 are the same, because both prophets "were moved by the Holy Spirit" as they prophesied. (2 Peter 1:21) Higher critics waste their time when they try to prove which writer was copying the other. "Professing themselves to be wise, they became fools." (Romans 1:22)

Jerusalem in the Time of Isaiah
Isaiah 2:5-9

O house of Jacob, come, and let us walk in the light of the LORD. 2:5 Isaiah now turns to the people of his own day and urges them to walk in the light of God, knowing that the kingdom of God would be established in the future. All nations would be blessed by the teachings and the peaceful examples of God's people. But Isaiah knows that his own people were not listening to the word of the LORD.

They are full of superstitions from the East; they practice divinations like the Philistines and clasp hands with pagans. 2:6 [NIV] Instead of being an example to the nations, they were following the sinful ways of other nations. Instead of trusting in God, they were trusting in their wealth. **2:7** Instead of worshiping the LORD, their land was full of idols. **2:8-9** As Christians, we must guard ourselves from following the sinful ways of the world and trusting in our material wealth. We are to be "the light of the world." (Matthew 5:14-16)

The Day of the LORD
Isaiah 2:10 – 4:1

Enter into the rock, and hide in the dust, for fear of the LORD and for the glory of his majesty. The lofty looks of man shall be humbled ... For the day of the LORD of hosts shall be upon everyone that is proud and lofty ... and he shall be brought down. 2:10-12 Sinful pride is having an undue regard for one's self, and it is involved in every sin. "Pride goes before destruction and a haughty spirit before a fall." (Prov. 16:18) We need to remember that "it is a fearful thing to fall into the hands of the living God." (Hebrews 10:32) "As I live," says the LORD, "every knee shall bow to me, and every tongue shall confess to God." (Romans 14:11; Isaiah 45:23)

The necessities of life, bread and water, will be taken away from Jerusalem and Judah "in that day." **3:1** All of their leaders will be taken away. **3:2-3** The people will oppress each other, neighbor against neighbor. Children will be disrespectful toward those that are older, and the indecent against the honorable. **3:5 Jerusalem is ruined, and Judah is fallen, because their tongue and their doings are against the LORD, to provoke the eyes of his glory. 3:8** Their destruction would be due to their spiritual and moral conditions that provoked God.

They were like Sodom; they were proud of their sin, and they did not hide it. **3:9** The righteous shall eat the fruit of their doings; but woe unto the wicked, for he will receive the wages of his sin. **3:10-11** "The wages of sin is death; but the gift of God is eternal life through Jesus Christ our Lord." (Romans 6:23) Galatians 6:7-8 warns, "Be not deceived! God is not mocked, for whatever a man sows that shall he also reap. For he that sows to his flesh shall of the flesh reap corruption; but he that sows to the Spirit shall of the Spirit reap life everlasting."

"As for my people, children are their oppressors, and women rule over them. O my people, they which lead you cause you to err and destroy the way of your paths." 3:12 They had mistreated the poor. **3:13-14** God would judge the wicked women of Jerusalem. **3:16 - 4:1** The nation suffers when its women lose their sense of proper conduct and compassion.

The Redeemed Jerusalem
Isaiah 4:2-6

In that day shall the Branch of the LORD be beautiful and glorious, and the fruit of the earth shall be excellent and comely for them that are escaped of Israel. 4:2 In verse 1, "in that day" refers to the day of the LORD's judgment. When the Assyrians came up against Judah, only a branch, a sprout, was left in Jerusalem. After the fall of Jerusalem and the captivity in Babylon, only a **remnant** would return to establish again the nation in Jerusalem. The LORD kept his promise to redeem Israel. He also kept his promise to David that his throne would be established forever (2 Samuel 7:8-13) by sending the Christ, who is called the Branch, "a rod out of the stem of Jesse" in Isaiah 11:1. In verse 2, "in that day" refers to the Christian Age, as it usually does in the prophets. God would cleanse and restore his people.

And it shall come to pass, that he that is left in Zion, and he that remains in Jerusalem, shall be called holy, even everyone that is written among the living in Jerusalem. 4:3 Zion is the New Jerusalem, which is entered only by those whose names are written in the Lamb's Book of Life. (Rev. 21:27) This is "the city of righteousness, the faithful city." (Isaiah 1:26) Those in this Jerusalem are holy – they are dedicated to the LORD.

The Parable of the Disappointing Vineyard
Isaiah 5:1-7

My well-beloved has a vineyard in a very fruitful hill. And he fenced it and gathered out the stones thereof and planted it with the choicest vine, and built a tower in the midst of it, and also made a winepress therein; and he looked that it should bring forth grapes, but it brought forth wild grapes. 5:1-2 "My well-beloved" is the LORD, who planted the house of Israel as his vineyard in the fruitful land of Palestine. He carefully prepared and protected his vineyard. But instead of having the good fruit that he desired, his vineyard became contaminated and produced wild grapes. The LORD asks, **"What could have been done more to my vineyard that I have not done in it?" 5:4** God was not responsible for Israel's sins and all the sufferings that they produced—the wild grapes. This is his verdict: **"I will tell you what I will do to my vineyard. I will take away the hedge** (the protection) **thereof, and it shall be eaten up; and break down the wall thereof, and it shall be trodden down. And I will lay it waste ... And I will command the clouds that they rain no rain upon it. For the vineyard of the LORD of hosts is the house of Israel, and the men of Judah his pleasant plant." 5:5-7** God would remove his blessing.

The Condemnation of Judah for its Sins
Isaiah 5:8-30

Woe unto them that join house to house, that lay field to field. 5:8 Because of covetousness, their great houses and the fields would be left desolate and useless.

Woe unto them that rise up early in the morning that they may follow strong drink, who continue until

night till wine inflames them. 5:11 Their purpose each day was to be intoxicated with strong drink from early morning till night. They had no time for God. **5:12**

Therefore, my people are gone into captivity, because they have no knowledge. 5:13 At this time, Hosea was saying to Israel. "There is no truth, nor mercy, nor knowledge of God in the land ... My people are destroyed for lack of knowledge." (Hosea 4:1, 6) This knowledge includes knowing God in a right relationship. Judah would go into exile in Babylon. Remember, God's word is so sure that he "calls those things which are not as though they were." (Romans 4:17)

Therefore, hell has enlarged herself and opened her mouth without measure. 5:14 *Sheol* is the word in the original language, and it means the grave. Death will devour a great number of those who have pomp and glory. **But the Lord of hosts shall be exalted in judgment. 5:16**

Woe unto them that draw iniquity with cords of vanity. 5:18 In their unbelief, they mocked God's word, saying, **"Let him make speed, and hasten his work that we may see it; and let the counsel of the Holy One of Israel draw near and come that we may know." 5:19**

Woe unto them that call evil good, and good evil; that put darkness for light, and light for darkness; that put bitter for sweet, and sweet for bitter. 5:20 Denying absolute truth is nothing new. Sinful unbelievers have always called evil good and good evil. They call their darkness "enlightenment;" and they call the light of God's truth "the ignorance of the dark ages." To them immoral living is sweet, and obeying God's moral law is bitter.

Woe unto them that are wise in their own eyes. 5:21 Wisdom begins with reverence for God. "The fear of the LORD is the beginning of wisdom; and the knowledge of the holy is understanding." (Proverbs 9:10)

Woe to them that are mighty to drink wine. 5:22 Drinking intoxicating drinks may make one feel mighty and great. But strong drink causes unclear thinking and uncontrolled actions. His drinking may cause him to hurt himself and others. Great men show their strength with thoughtful words and helpful deeds.

Woe unto them ... which justify the wicked for reward. 5:23 Those that pervert justice for a bribe will receive the judgment of God. (Ex. 23:8; Deut. 27:25)

They have cast away the law of the LORD of hosts and despised the word of the Holy One of Israel. Therefore, the anger of the LORD is kindled against his people, and he has stretched forth his hand against them. 5:24, 25 The reason for God's anger was their rejection of his word. This is still true today. Jesus said, "He that rejects me and receives not my words has one that judges him; the word that I have spoken shall judge him in the last day." (John 12:48)

And he will lift up an ensign to the nations ... and, behold they shall come with speed swiftly. 5:27 God would use the other nations to punish his people. He would use Assyria and then Babylon. **Their roaring shall be like a lion, they shall roar like young lions: yea they shall roar and lay hold of the prey and shall carry it away ... and none shall deliver it. 5:29-30** The conquering nation is compared to a lion. The symbol of Babylon was a lion. (Daniel 7:1-4; cf. Daniel 2:36-40) The Jews would be carried away to Babylon.

Review Questions on Isaiah 1 – 5

1. "The _____ knows its owner, and the _____ its master's crib; but _____ does not know." 1:3

2. Isaiah describes the "sinful nation as a people laden with _____, a seed of _____." 1:4

3. Jerusalem would be left as a _____ in a garden of cucumbers, as a _____ city. 1:8

4. "Cease to do _____. Learn to do _____." 1:16, 17

5. "Though your _____ are as scarlet, they shall be white as snow." 1:18

6. "If you are _____ and _____, you shall eat the good of the land." 1:19

7. "How has the faithful city become a _____!" 1:21 "Afterward you shall be called the city of righteousness, the _____ city." 1:26

8. The _____ is the New Jerusalem, the holy city, in Revelation 21:2-10.

9. The promise in Isaiah 2:2 that the mountain of the Lord's house shall be established "in the last days" was fulfilled on the day of _____.

10. Isaiah predicted that "all _____ shall flow unto it…for out of _____ shall go forth the law, and the word of the Lord from _____." 2:2, 3

Charges Against Jerusalem

11. Isaiah pleaded with his people, "O house of Jacob, come, and let us walk in the _____ of the LORD." 2:5

12. His people were following other _____;
    the object of their trust was their _____;
    and their land was full of _____. 2:6-8

13. What was coming "upon everyone that is proud"? 2:12 _____

14. From Jerusalem and from Judah would be taken away the whole stay (supply) of _____ and _____. 3:1

15. Jerusalem and Judah were like _____, because they were proud of their sin and did not hide it. 3:9

16. "In that day shall the _____ of the LORD be beautiful and glorious." 4:2

17. "He that remains in Jerusalem shall be called _____, even everyone that is _____ among the living in Jerusalem." 4:3

18. In Isaiah 5:1-7, The house of Israel is compared to a disappointing _____.

19. "Woe unto them that call evil _____, and good _____." 5:20

20. "Woe unto them that are _____ in their own eyes." 5:21 "They have cast away the _____ of the LORD." 5:24

The Coming of Immanuel
Isaiah 6 – 9

"Behold, the virgin shall conceive and bear a Son, and shall call His name Immanuel."
Isaiah 7:14 NKJV

The Call of Isaiah to be God's Prophet
Isaiah 6

The previous chapters provide the setting for the call of Isaiah in chapter six. He would be God's spokesman predicting the coming of the Messiah. His people are being punished for their sins, but Isaiah also promises the way of salvation. In chapter 7, the prophet predicts the virgin birth of Immanuel, whose name means, "God with us." He will be called, "Wonderful, Counselor, The Mighty God, The Everlasting Father, and the Prince of Peace." (9:2-6)

In the year that king Uzziah died, I saw also the Lord sitting upon a throne, high and lifted up, and his train filled the temple. 6:1 This vision was before the death of Uzziah, because Isaiah prophesied "in the days of Uzziah." (1:1) The vision came during a time when Isaiah was saddened by the fallen condition of his cousin, King Uzziah. The kingdom of Judah had prospered greatly during the fifty-two-year reign of Uzziah. He had trusted in the LORD, and God blessed him. However, toward the end of his reign, his pride caused him to disregard God's law. He entered the temple to burn incense, which was the exclusive duty of the priests. For his transgression and impenitence, God struck him with leprosy, and he lived in an isolated house until the day of his death. (2 Chronicles 26:16-21)

Angels called **seraphim** were praising God, saying, **"Holy, Holy, Holy, is the Lord of hosts; the whole earth is full of his glory." 6:2-3** God, comprised of three persons with one divine nature, has the greatest degree of holiness. God's glory can be seen throughout the earth in the design and beauty of his creation. (Romans 1:19-20) He is "upholding all things by the word of his power." (Hebrews 1:3) Shackelford says that "glory expresses the presence and protection of God. When God's glory departed from Jerusalem (Ezekiel 11:23), the city was left unprotected. When His glory returned (Ezekiel 43:2-5), God's presence and protection were evident." [6]

And the posts of the door moved at the voice of him that cried, and the house was filled with smoke. 6:4 The smoke symbolizes "the glory of God and his power." (cf. Revelation 15:8) **Then I said, "Woe is me! for I am undone; because I am a man of unclean lips, and I dwell in the midst of a people of unclean lips for my eyes have seen the King, the Lord of hosts." 6:5** Everyone that comes into the presence of God feels reverential fear and his own unworthiness and sinfulness. Isaiah was like Moses at the burning bush (Exodus 3:6, 11), and Peter who saw the great power of Jesus at the great catch of fish (Luke 5:9-10), and all the other apostles when Jesus calmed the stormy sea (Mark 5:40-41). When we see God in his holiness, greatness and glory, we are able to see ourselves as we really are: unclean sinners in need of God's grace and mercy.

Then one of the angels touched Isaiah's mouth with a live coal from the altar and said, **"Your iniquity is taken away, and your sin purged." 6:6-7** Isaiah was forgiven because, in the future, the blood of Jesus would atone for his sins. Jesus' death on the cross was necessary for the

---

[6] Don Shackelford, *Truth for Today Commentary, Isaiah*, p. 94

redemption of sins under the first covenant. (Hebrews 9:11-15) **Also, I heard the voice of the Lord, saying, "Whom shall I send, and who will go for us?" Then I said, "Here I am, send me." 6:8** Isaiah volunteered to be God's messenger. He had seen the divine Word in his glory (John 1:1-18; 12:39-41) and knew his own need for forgiveness. He was ready to take God's message of salvation to his sinful nation. When we know our need of a Savior, then we'll be able to lead others to Christ.

The Lord was using *irony* when he instructed Isaiah, **"Go and tell this people, 'Hear indeed, but understand not; see indeed, but perceive not.'" 6:9** The people had sarcastically expressed their eagerness to see God's works and hear his counsel in 5:19. God is describing their condition in 6:9-10. He had given them his word, but they refused to listen; he had shown them his works, but they had closed their eyes. This is the meaning given by Jesus to this passage in Matthew 13:14-15.

Isaiah asks, **"Lord, how long?"** How long will the people continue rejecting God's warnings? God answers, **"Until the cities are wasted and without inhabitant and the houses without man, and the land is utterly desolate." 6:11** Their refusal to listen to the LORD would result in the destruction of their cities and their exile in Babylon.

"But yet a tenth will be in it, and will return and be for consuming, as a terebinth tree or as an oak, whose stump remains when it is cut down. So, the holy seed shall be its stump." 6:13 ^{NKJV} Homer Hailey explains, "Though a tenth, a small remnant, escape, even it in turn will be eaten up until those that remain will be but a remnant of the remnant ... the stump; so, the holy seed is the substance or life thereof. The thought is that out of the small remnant escaping will come a smaller remnant;

even the whole remnant shall not endure. This smaller remnant, the stock or substance of the remnant, is what Paul had in view when he said, 'Even so then at this present time also there is a remnant according to the election of grace' (Rom. 11:5; also see 9:27-28)." [7]

And it came to pass in the days of Ahaz the son Jotham, the son of Uzziah, king of Judah, that Rezin the king of Syria and Pekah the king of Israel went up toward Jerusalem to war against it but could not prevail against it. 7:1 The wonderful prophecy of the virgin birth of Jesus came at a time when the kingdom of Judah was surrounded by enemies.

Ahaz king of Judah was a wicked idolater who made images for worshiping the Baals and sacrificed his sons in the Valley of Hinnom. Therefore, the LORD delivered him into the hand of the king of Syria, who carried away a great number of captives to Damascus. At the same time, the king of Israel smote Judah with a great slaughter. (2 Chron. 28:1-5) Also, the Edomites had carried away captives from Judah, and the Philistines invaded cities in lowlands and southern parts of Judah. (2 Chron. 28:17) Judah was surrounded by enemies. Ahaz sent to Assyria for help, but Tiglath-Pileser king of Assyria came and carried away things from the temple but did not help him. (2 Chron. 28:16, 20-21) Instead of repenting of his sins, Ahaz began sacrificing to the gods of Damascus because he thought they were stronger than the LORD God of Israel. (2 Chron. 28:22-25)

Rezin the king of Syria and Pekah king of Israel formed a coalition to make war against Jerusalem in order to replace Ahaz as king. **7:2, 6** When Ahaz heard of this plot, he was afraid. (2 Chronicles 28:5)

---

[7] Homer Hailey, *A Commentary on Isaiah*, p. 79

God sent Isaiah out to meet Ahaz. Isaiah was instructed to take with him his son **Shear-Jashub,** whose name means "a remnant will return." **7:3** Isaiah was to tell Ahaz, **"Take heed and be quiet; fear not, neither be fainthearted for the two tails of these smoking firebrands." 7:4** The plot of Syria and Israel would not be successful. **7:7** Ephraim (Israel) would cease being a people within sixty-five years. **7:8**. This prophecy was fulfilled after the fall of Israel, when the few Israelites that remained intermarried with the foreign immigrants.

Through Isaiah, **the LORD spoke again unto Ahaz, saying, "Ask a sign of the LORD thy God." 7:10-11** The LORD wanted to show his power over the gods of Syria that Ahaz was worshiping.

But Ahaz said, "I will not ask, neither will I tempt the LORD." 7:13 The Law does teach, "You shall not tempt the LORD your God," (Deuteronomy 16:18) But the king was only pretending to have respect for God. To ask for this sign would have shown faith in the LORD. No one tempts God when they do what he has commanded. Ahaz refused to ask for a sign because he had made up his mind to go to the king of Assyria for help, instead of trusting in God, who had promised David that his kingdom and throne would be "established forever." (2 Samuel 7:16)

Isaiah said, **"Hear now, O house of David, is it a small thing for you to weary men, but will you weary my God, also?" 7:13** The LORD was Isaiah's God, but not Ahaz's god. Ahaz had rejected the LORD for idols. He was wearying God by not trusting his power.

"Therefore, the Lord himself will give you a sign. Behold, the virgin shall conceive and bear a son, and shall call his name Immanuel." 7:14 ᴱˢⱽ The Hebrew word *almah,* that is translated "virgin," means a young unmarried woman of good moral character. She is **the virgin;** the definite article is in the Hebrew text. The prophecy is about a particular woman, not just any woman. The virgin-birth prophecy is applied only to Mary giving birth to Jesus, according to the inspired commentary of Matthew 1:22-23. She will call her son's name **Immanuel**, meaning "God with us." The Lord would give the house of David and the nation a sign. The word "you" is plural. While Ahaz feared that his kingdom would be overthrown by Syria and Israel, the LORD was promising the coming of the Christ who would establish the throne of David forever. Isaiah had already predicted Christ's kingdom in 2:2-4. Now in Isaiah 7:14, the prophet says the virgin will bear a son, who will be called "God with us." More is said about the birth of this son in Isaiah 9:6-7, "His name shall be called, Wonderful, Counsellor, The Mighty God, The Everlasting Father, The Prince of Peace.'" The description of his reign is in Isaiah 11. The prophet Micah, who also was prophesying at this time, predicted that Bethlehem would be the birth place of the Christ, "whose goings forth have been from everlasting." (Micah 5:2) The Messiah would not be an ordinary man; he would be deity from eternity. God would be with us!

"For before the child shall know to refuse the evil and choose the good, the land that you abhor shall be forsaken of both her kings." 7:16 Shackelford says, "For Ahaz, the sign was only a space of time. By the time a woman could conceive and give birth to a son, and that son could grow to a knowledgeable age, the two kings that he feared would be gone." [8]

The LORD shall bring upon you and upon your people and upon your father's house, days that have not come, from the day that Ephraim departed from

---

[8] Don Shackelford, Ibid., p. 115

Judah—even the king of Assyria. 7:17-25** The king of Assyria, whose help Ahaz was seeking, would indeed conquer Syria and Israel. (2 Kings 17:1-18) However, the Assyrians would continue their conquests into Judah, destroying its fortified cities and besieging even the city of Jerusalem. (2 Kings 18:13-19:37)

Then the L{ORD} said to me, "Take a large tablet and write on it in common characters, 'Belonging to Maher-Shalal-Hash-Baz.'" 8:1** ESV In the presence of two faithful witnesses, Isaiah wrote with a stylus on a large clay tablet these Hebrew words that are translated: *"Speed the Spoil, Hasten the Booty."* **8:2

When Isaiah's wife **conceived and bore a son,** the L{ORD} said, **"Call his name Maher-Shalal-Hash-Baz. For before the child shall have knowledge to cry 'My father,' and 'My mother,' the riches of Damascus and the spoil of Samaria will be taken away before the king of Assyria." 8:3-4** Shackelford states, "In fact, just two years after the time of this prediction, it was fulfilled. Tiglath-Pileser III of Assyria deported the people of Israel (represented by the capital, Samaria) in 733 B.C. He besieged and plundered Damascus (the capital of Syria) in 732 B.C. The king could easily verify the accuracy of Isaiah's message." [9]

"This people refuse the waters of Shiloah that go softly and rejoice in Rezin and Remaliah's son." 8:6 The waters of Shiloah were the source of Jerusalem's water supply, and they represented the L{ORD}, their source of life. Instead of trusting in God, the people were rejoicing because the Assyrians had killed Rezin king of Syria (2 Kings 16:7-9) and Remaliah's son, Pekah king of Israel, was humbled when captives from Samaria were led away to Assyria. (2 Kings 15:9) These were Judah's

---

[9] Don Shackelford, Ibid., p. 119

enemies at this time. Hailey observes, "That jubilance would be short-lived, for the very power that had overrun Israel and Syria would soon overflow Judah." [10]

"Now therefore, behold, the Lord brings up upon them the waters of the River, strong and many, even the king of Assyria, and all his glory; and he shall ... go over all his banks." 8:7 The invasion of the land of Judah by the king of Assyria is compared with the mighty flood waters of the Euphrates River. The Jews would not be totally conquered, because the flood waters would only reach up **to the neck. 8:8** The nation would be spared total destruction because this is Immanuel's land, the land where the Christ would be born. The alliances among nations will be broken; their plots against the Lord's people will come to nothing, because Immanuel, "God with us," will accomplish his purpose. Psalm 2:1 asks, "Why do the heathen rage and the people image a vain thing? ... He that sits in the heavens shall laugh; the LORD shall have them in derision." (Psalm 2: 4) This Psalm is fulfilled in Christ. (Acts 4:24-30; Acts 13:32-33; Heb. 1:5)

The LORD spoke thus to me with a strong hand and instructed me that I should not walk in the way of this people, saying: "Do not say, 'A conspiracy,' concerning all that this people call a conspiracy, nor be afraid of their threats, nor be troubled." 8:11-12 NKJV Today, we need to obey these same instructions. We should not fear what the unbelievers fear. "For God has not given us the spirit of fear; but of power, and of love, and of a sound mind." (2 Tim. 1:7)

"Sanctify the LORD of hosts himself and let him be your fear, and let him be your dread." 8:13 We should have a holy reverence for God. Peter has the same message for us, "If you suffer for righteousness' sake, happy are you; and be not afraid of their terror, neither be

---

[10] Homer Hailey, Ibid., p. 94

troubled. But sanctify the Lord God in your hearts and be ready always to give an answer to every man that asks you a reason of the hope that is in you with meekness and fear." (1 Peter 3:14-15) **And he shall be for a sanctuary. 8:14** For believers God is a **sanctuary**, a holy place, a place of refuge and protection. For unbelievers, God is a **stone** over which they will stumble, fall, and be broken.

Bind up the testimony; seal the law among my disciples. 8:16 Shackelford says that this "refers to the ancient custom of rolling or wrapping a written scroll and placing a seal on it to ensure its authenticity and safeguard it from tampering." [11] Homer Hailey suggests that the LORD is speaking through the prophet to his disciples to bind the teaching of this chapter in their hearts.[12] Isaiah says, **"And I will wait upon the LORD." 8:17** Isaiah would patiently wait for God to fulfill his prophecies.

Behold, I and the children whom the LORD has given me are for signs and for wonders in Israel. 8:18 Isaiah's name means "The LORD Saves." His son Shear-Jashub's name means "A Remnant Will Return." Maher-Shalal-Hash-Baz means "Speed the Spoil, Hasten the Booty" and describes the defeat of Israel and Syria by the Assyrians.

And when they say to you, "Seek those who are mediums and wizards," ... should not a people seek their God? Should they seek the dead, on behalf of the living? To the law and to the testimony: if they speak not according to this word, it is because there is no light in them." 8:19-20 God's people should be guided by God's word, which equips us for life and godliness and every good work. (2 Peter 1:3 and 2 Timothy 3:15-17)

---

[11] Don Shackelford, Ibid., p.123
[12] Homer Hailey, Ibid., p. 97

The people that walked in darkness have seen a great light. 9:2 This verse predicts the coming of Christ (Matthew 4:12-16), who is "the true Light" (John 1:9).

For unto us a Child is born, unto us a Son is given; and the government shall be upon his shoulder. And his name shall be called Wonderful, Counselor, The Mighty God, The Everlasting Father, The Prince of Peace. And of the increase of his government and peace there shall be no end, upon the throne of David, and upon his kingdom to order and to establish it with judgment and justice. 9:6-7 Unto us a Child is born— "The Word became flesh and dwelt among us" (John 1:14); unto us a Son is given—"God so loved the world that he gave his only begotten Son" to die on the cross so "that whosoever believes in him should not perish but have everlasting life." (John 3:16) His judgment will be upon the unbelievers and the wicked. **9:8-21**

Review Questions on Isaiah 6 – 9

1. Isaiah was called to be a prophet in the year that king _____ died. 6:1-8

2. When the LORD asked, "Whom shall I send, and who will go for us," what was Isaiah's response? 6:8 _____

3. Ahaz was king of _____, Rezin was the king of _____, and Pekah king of _____. 7:1

4. What was causing Ahaz to fear? 7:5-6
   _____
   _____

5. The name of Isaiah's oldest son was Shear-Jashub, which means _____.

6. What sign did the LORD give to King Ahaz? 7:14
   _____
   _____

7. For Ahaz, the sign was a _____ of _____.

8. For the future, it was a sign that the _____ would be born of a _____.

9. The name *Immanuel* means _____.

10. What name did God give Isaiah's new son? 8:3
    _____

11. What does this name mean?
    _____

12. Why was this son given this name? 8:4
_____
_____

13. "The waters of Shiloah" represent _____, the source of life. 8:6

14. What did the flood waters of the Euphrates River represent? 8:7 _____

15. Because the land of Judah would be the birthplace of Christ it is called _____ land. 8:8

16. "Sanctify the _____ of hosts himself; let him be your _____ and let him be your _____." 8:13

17. "Bind up the _____, seal the _____ among my disciples." 8:16

18. A people should seek their God and not _____ and _____. 8:19

19. "The people who walked in _____ have seen a great _____." 9:2

20. "For unto us a _____ is born, unto us a _____ is given." 9:6

21. What five names will the Christ be called? 9:6
_____
_____

22. "Of the increase of his government and peace there shall be ____ _____." 9:7

The Peaceful Kingdom
Isaiah 10 – 12

In these chapters, the LORD promises the coming of the peaceful kingdom of the Branch of Jesse. However, before its coming, things will look hopeless. God will use Assyria to punish the kingdoms of Israel and of Judah for their sins. Israel will be destroyed, and its people scattered among the nations. Even in Judah, only a remnant will be left in Jerusalem. Then God will punish the Assyrians, the rod of his anger, for the arrogant heart of its king. In the future, a remnant of all of God's people will return to the LORD and enjoy the peaceful kingdom.

"Woe unto them that decree unrighteous decrees." 10:1 God punishes rulers that misuse their power and issue "unrighteous decrees." Judges took bribes and robbed the poor of justice. **"What will you do in the day of visitation and in the desolation, which shall come from afar? To whom will you flee for help?" 10:3** They themselves would be helpless when the Assyrian army invaded the kingdom of Judah.

"Woe to Assyria, the rod of My anger ... I will send him against an ungodly nation and against the people of My wrath." 10:5, 6 NKJV God was using Assyria to punish his people Israel. But the Assyrians thought that they were successful in defeating other nations because of their military power. Their king would say that as he had done to Samaria, he would do to Jerusalem. **10:7-11** He did not understand that he was only a rod to carry out God's purpose.

The LORD will say, **"I will punish the fruit of the arrogant heart of the king of Assyria, and the glory of his haughty looks. For he says, 'By the strength of my**

hand I have done it, and by my wisdom ... also I have removed the boundaries of the people.'" 10:12-13 NKJV God showed the king of Assyria who was ruling over the nations. The angel of the LORD slew 185,000 in the Assyrian camp in one night, and the king of Assyria was killed by two of his sons after he returned to his home in Nineveh. (Isaiah 37:36-38) This "marked the beginning of the end of Assyrian glory and might. In less than a century, Assyria would be no more." [13]

Shall the axe boast itself against him that hews therewith? 10:15 On its own, the ax is powerless. Assyria was only God's axe of wrath; the power belonged to God. **Therefore, the Lord of hosts shall send leanness among his fat ones; and under his glory he shall kindle a burning like the burning of a fire. And the light of Israel shall be for a fire. 10:16-17** After God was through using the Assyrians to punish Israel and Judah, this arrogant nation would suffer scarcity and be consumed by a fire. God is described as "an everlasting light" in Isaiah 60:19 and as "a consuming fire" in Deuteronomy 4:14. The burning started when the LORD smote the Assyrian army besieging Jerusalem (Isaiah 37) and completely consumed the nation when Nineveh fell to the Babylonians in 612 BC.

And it shall come to pass in that day, that the remnant of Israel and such as are escaped of the house of Jacob ... shall stay upon the LORD, the Holy One of Israel, in truth. The remnant shall return, even the remnant of Jacob, unto the mighty God. 10:20-21 Shackelford says, "The remnant of Israel is introduced for the first time, although it was alluded to in Isaiah's call (6:13). The idea of the remnant also appears in the name of Isaiah's son Shear-Jashub (7:3), whose name means **a remnant will return.**" [14] The remnant is composed of

---

[13] Don Shackelford, *Truth for Today Commentary--Isaiah*, p. 148
[14] Don Shackelford, Ibid., p.149

those that rely upon the LORD; they put their trust and hope in God, not in a world power. After the Assyrians destroyed the kingdom of Israel and besieged the city of Jerusalem, only a remnant was left in Judah, including Hezekiah king of Judah. (Isaiah 37:14-20)

For though your people Israel are as the sand of the sea, yet a remnant of them shall return. 10:22 In comparison to the entire nation of Israel, the remnant would be small in number. After the destruction decreed by God to punish his people by the Assyrians and by the Babylonians, only a few of them returned to Jerusalem, including some from the kingdom of Israel. When baby Jesus was presented at the temple, Anna the prophetess gave thanks and spoke of him as the Redeemer. She was of the tribe of Asher in the kingdom of Israel. (Luke 2:36) Only a remnant of the remnant that returned to Jerusalem would be saved with the coming of the Christ, in whom is overflowing righteousness. Homer Hailey wrote that the Lord "never promised that all the descendants of Abraham would be saved; those who would be saved were always spoken of as a remnant." [15] This passage is quoted in Romans 9:27 and applied to those whom the Lord has called, "not of the Jews only, but also of the Gentiles." (Romans 9:24) The kingdom of Israel became part of the Gentiles, according to Amos 9:9 and Hosea 8:8.

"O my people that dwell in Zion, be not afraid of the Assyrian; he shall smite you with a rod." 10:24 The faithful remnant in Jerusalem should not be afraid when the Assyrians besieged their city. **"For yet a very little while, and the indignation shall cease." 10:25** God's punishment of Judah by the Assyrians would be for a short time, and then the suffering would be over.

---

[15] Homer Hailey, *A Commentary on Isaiah*, p. 117

And the LORD of hosts shall stir up a scourge for him according to the slaughter of Midian at the rock of Oreb; and as his rod was upon the sea. And it shall come to pass in that day that his burden shall be taken away. 10:26, 27 Israel was greatly outnumbered by the Midianites, but God used Gideon and only 300 to initiate a great victory in Judges 7:7-25. The rock of Oreb is the place where a prince of the Midianites was killed. When things looked hopeless at the Red Sea, God destroyed the Egyptian army when Moses lifted his rod. The advance of the Assyrian army is described in **10:28-32**. But the LORD would have the victory!

The Peaceful Kingdom
Isaiah 11

And there shall come forth a rod out of the stem of Jesse, and a Branch shall grow out of his roots. 11:1 From the time of Ahaz, the kings of Judah were under the influence of other nations. They had to pay tribute to them. After the fall of Jerusalem in 586 BC, the Jews would be without a king from the lineage of David. The only thing left would be "the stem of Jesse." But the Messiah would come out of this stump of the family tree. Don Shackelford writes: "We might expect that David, not his father Jesse, would be 'the stem.' However, the intended reference may not be to another king in the lineage of David, but to another 'David'." [16] Homer Hailey adds, "Neither the Branch nor His kingdom would be identical in nature with the old Davidic order ... Anything human is destined to corruption and decay. The new spiritual kingdom and its divine King (7:14, 9:6-7) would be subject to neither."[17] The Messiah is also referred to as the "Branch" in Jeremiah 23:5, Zechariah 3:8, and Zechariah 6:12.

---

[16] Don Shackelford, Ibid., p. 158
[17] Homer Hailey, Ibid., p. 120

And the Spirit of the LORD shall rest upon him, the spirit of wisdom and understanding, the spirit of counsel and might, the spirit of knowledge and the fear of the LORD. 11:2 The Holy Spirit descended upon Jesus at his baptism. (Mark 1:10) Jesus possessed the qualifications of a ruler in absolute perfection. Wisdom is the application of understanding. Counsel is the ability to plan a solution; and might is the power to carry it out.

His delight is in the fear of the LORD. 11:3 NKJV "The fear of the LORD is the beginning of knowledge." (Proverbs 1:7) His reverent fear will cause him to rule in submission to God's will. Jesus said, "I came down from heaven, not to do my own will, but the will of him that sent me." (John 6:38) "For I always do those things that please him." (John 8:29)

He shall not judge after the sight of his eyes; neither reprove after the hearing of his ears. But with righteousness shall he judge the poor and reprove with equity for the meek of the earth, and he shall smite the earth with the rod of his mouth, and with the breath of his lips shall he slay the wicked. 11:3-4 Christ does not judge according to appearance or hearsay, but he judges impartially with righteous judgment. (John 7:24) His words will judge us in the last day. (John 12:48)

"The wolf also shall dwell with the lamb, and the leopard shall lie down with the kid (young goat)**, the calf and the young lion and the fatling together; and a little child shall lead them." 11:6-8** This is a figurative description of the peaceful nature of Messiah's kingdom. Former enemies will be at peace with one another in his church. His "perfect love casts out fear." (1 John 4:18) **"They shall not hurt nor destroy in all my holy mountain, for the earth shall be full of the knowledge of the LORD, as the waters cover the sea." 11:9** God's "holy mountain" in Isaiah 2:2-4 is his spiritual kingdom, the church. The LORD brings peace. Christ is called the Prince of Peace in Isaiah 9:6.

"In that day, there shall be a root of Jesse, which shall stand for an ensign of the people, to it shall the Gentiles seek, and his rest shall be glorious. 11:10 Christ, the root of Jesse, would come and set up his peaceable kingdom, the church, where "they shall beat their swords into plowshares." (Isaiah 2:4) The Messiah would be like a banner, around which the people of all nations would gather. (Rom. 15:9-12) They will enjoy a glorious resting place in heaven. (Matt. 11:28; Rev. 21:1 – 22:5)

And it shall come to pass in that day, that the LORD shall set his hand again the second time to recover the remnant of his people, which shall be left. 11:11 Hailey explains, "The first time God set His hand to recover the remnant involved the Jews under Zerubbabel and Joshua the high priest from captivity in Babylon (see Ezra 1-6). Now in that day—the day of the reigning Branch—He would set His hand a second time to recover the remnant from all parts of the earth. Under the gospel God has been doing this since Pentecost (Acts 2). Paul says, 'Even so then at this present time also there is a remnant according to the election of grace.' (Romans 11:5) This remnant according to the election of grace is being called and gathered under the rule of Him who rose from the root of Jesse (Romans 15:12)." [18]

And he shall set up an ensign for the nations, and shall assemble the outcasts of Israel, and gather the dispersed of Judah from the four corners of the earth. 11:12 The "outcasts" of Israel had become part of the Gentiles (Hosea 8:8, Amos 9:9), but in Christ they are reunited with the Jews, who also were scattered

---

[18] Homer Hailey, Ibid., pp. 124-125

throughout the world. Christ's gospel is the ensign that brings people together in one body, the church. (Ephesians 1:10, 22-23; 3:1-6) He reconciles both Jews and Gentiles "to God in one body through the cross" by the gospel of "peace." (Ephesians 2:11-17)

Ephraim shall not envy Judah, and Judah shall not vex Ephraim. 11:13 Ephraim stands for the entire nation of Israel. Shackelford says, "The **remnant** of the tribes would no longer fight each other but would join forces to defeat their common enemies (vv. 13, 14). It is later revealed that a physical warfare is not intended here; rather, the prophet was speaking of a spiritual conflict. It was to be led by 'the root of Jesse.' This great victory would be reminiscent of **Israel's** deliverance from **Egypt** (vv. 15, 16)." [19]

And there shall be a highway for the remnant of his people, which shall be left. 11:16 This is not a physical highway but a spiritual road that the redeemed will travel. Isaiah 35:8-10, reveals, "A highway shall be there, and it shall be called the way of holiness; the unclean shall not pass over it." (cf. John 14:6)

A Hymn of Thanksgiving and Praise
Isaiah 12

And in that day you shall say: "O LORD, I will praise you; though you were angry with me, your anger is turned away, and you comfort me." 12:1 The phrase, "in that day," refers to the time of the Messiah. Individuals of the remnant will no longer be identified by their nationality. They will praise God for comforting them in the peaceful kingdom.

---

[19] Don Shackelford, Ibid., p. 161

"Behold, God is my salvation, I will trust and not be afraid." 12:2 King Ahaz had failed to learn this great lesson. (2 Kings 16) King Hezekiah is a great example of one who lived by this truth. (2 Kings 18-19)

Therefore, with joy you shall draw water out of the wells of salvation. 12:3 Shackelford notes, "Water is a beautiful figure of salvation to those who live in an arid land such as Palestine. The Jews of Jesus' day had a ceremony based on this verse. During the Feast of Tabernacles, they would march to the pool of Siloam and fill a golden pitcher with water. As they returned to the temple, they chanted this verse. They poured out the water by the altar as a figure of their salvation." [20]

And in that day you shall say: "Praise the LORD, call upon his name; declare his doings among the peoples, make mention that his name is exalted." 12:4 Christians should praise and exalt the name of our Lord Jesus Christ and tell others about the great things he has done. (Mark 5:19)

Sing unto the LORD, for he has done excellent things; this is known in all the earth. 12:5 We are able to teach and encourage one another by singing songs. (Colossians 3:16-17) In Christ's kingdom, we are to praise God for his wonderful works with singing.

Cry out and shout, you inhabitant of Zion, for great is the Holy One of Israel in your midst! 12:6 Christ is now with his church, spiritual Mount Zion, and he has promised to be with us always. (Heb. 12:22-23) The redeemed will be with him in heaven and will be singing a new song before God's throne. (Rev. 14:1-5)

---

[20] Don Shackelford, Ibid., p. 165

Review Questions on Isaiah 10 – 12

1. "Woe unto them that decree _____ decrees." 10:1

2. "Woe to _____, the _____ of My anger." 10:5 NKJV

3. "I will punish the fruit of the _____ heart of the king of Assyria." 10:12 NKJV

4. "Shall the axe _____ itself against him that hews therewith?" 10:15

5. Upon whom will **the remnant** rely? 10:20
   _____

6. Those who would be saved were always spoken of as a _____.

7. A rod shall come forth out of the stem of _____ and a _____ shall grow out of his roots. 11:1

8. The "Branch" is symbolic for the _____.

9. The promise, "The Spirit of the Lord will rest on Him," was fulfilled when the _____ came upon Jesus at his _____.

10. The Branch will judge with _____.

11. What is represented figuratively by the wolf living with the lamb? 11:6 _____

12. "They shall not _____ nor _____ in all my holy mountain." 11:9

13. God's "holy mountain" is his _____.

14. "The earth shall be full of the _____ of the LORD as the waters cover the sea." 11:9

15. "For the _____ shall seek Him, and his resting place shall be glorious." 11:10 NKJV

16. The first time God recovered the remnant of his people was when the Jews returned to Jerusalem from _____.

17. God has been recovering his remnant for a second time from all of the earth since _____.

18. The outcasts of Israel were part of the _____.

19. The "highway for the remnant" is a _____ road that the _____ will travel. 11:16

20. A Hymn of _____ and _____ is in Isaiah 12.

21. "Behold, God is my _____; I will _____ and not be afraid." 12:2

22. In New Testament times, the words of Isaiah 12:3 were chanted by the people during the Feast of the _____.

God Judges the Nations
Isaiah 13 – 20

The kingdom of Judah is not to fear other nations, because God will punish those who oppress his people. God rules over all the kingdoms of the earth, and he will not tolerate their sins. Therefore, Judah should not make alliances with other nations.

The Prophecy against Babylon
Isaiah 13:1 – 14:23

The burden of Babylon which Isaiah the son of Amoz saw. 13:1 In prophecy, a **burden** is a judicial sentence. At the time of Isaiah, Babylon was not yet a world power, but it was increasing in military might. In the future, Babylon would destroy Jerusalem and the temple of God and exile the Jews from their homeland. God is passing his judgment against this proud and profane nation.

The noise of a multitude in the mountains, like as of a great people; a tumultuous noise of the kingdoms of nations gathered together; the LORD of hosts musters the host of the battle. 13:4 In prophecy, *mountains* represent kingdoms. This verse is describing the battle of Armageddon (Rev. 16:16) that occurs many times as "the day of the Lord," when God judges nations.

Howl, for the day of the LORD is at hand; it shall come as destruction from the Almighty. 13:6 God has foreknowledge. He could look into the future and see the proud Babylonian Empire and predict its death. He describes in figurative language his judgment upon the Babylonians: **the stars of heaven and the constellations thereof shall not give their light; the sun shall be darkened and the moon shall not cause her light to**

shine. And I will punish the world for their evil, and the wicked for their iniquity; and I will cause the arrogance of the proud to cease and will lay low the haughtiness of the terrible. 13:10 Babylon represents the ungodly society of the world that will be destroyed at the end of time. (Revelation 17-19)

Behold, I will stir up the Medes against them. 13:17 Isaiah predicted that God would use the Medes to punish Babylon. The Medes and Persians conquered Babylon in 539 BC, and the kingdom of Babylon was no more.

Babylon, the glory of kingdoms, the beauty of the Chaldeans' excellency, shall be as when God overthrew Sodom and Gomorrah. It shall never be inhabited. 13:19, 20 The attitude of Babylon toward its achievements make it a proper symbol for the humanistic society of the world. The Hanging Gardens of Babylon were one of the ancient world's Seven Wonders. Babylon's kingdom fell in 539 BC, but the city was not destroyed or deserted at that time. Alexander the Great died in Babylon in 323 BC. The city decayed gradually. Babylon became a deserted place in the third century AD.

For the LORD will have mercy on Jacob, and will yet choose Israel, and set them in their own land; and the strangers shall be joined with them, and they shall cleave to the house of Jacob. 14:1 This promise is to all of Israel and to the other nations that would join them. Abraham, Isaac, and Jacob desired "a better country, that is, a heavenly" country. (Hebrews 11:9, 16) They were promised, "In your seed shall all the nations of the earth be blessed." (Genesis 22:18; 26:4; 28:14) The Seed is Christ. (Galatians 3:16) The blessing of the promise is the forgiveness of sins. (Acts 2:38-39; Acts 3:25-26), and the land is heaven (Revelation 7:9-17).

And they shall take them captives, whose captives they were. 14:2 Shackelford explains, "At no time in her history did Israel possess the nations as an inheritance, as might have been expected from verse 2. This may be seen as a messianic statement of the conditions that find their fulfillment in the church." [21] In 2 Corinthians 10:4-5, Paul wrote, "The weapons we fight with are not weapons of the world. On the contrary, they have divine power to demolish strongholds. We demolish arguments and every pretension that sets itself up against the knowledge of God, and we take captive every thought to make it obedient to Christ." NIV

It shall come to pass in the day that the LORD shall give you rest from your sorrow, and from your fear, and from the hard bondage wherein you were made to serve, that you shall take up this proverb against the king of Babylon, and say, "How has the oppressor ceased! The LORD has broken the staff of the wicked, the scepter of the rulers." 14:3-5 The Babylonians were replaced by the Persian Empire, which let its subjects worship their own gods and keep their own customs. This tolerance won the loyalty of the conquered people. The LORD rules over the nations.

"How you are fallen from heaven, O Lucifer, son of the morning!" 14:12 Lucifer means "day star." This is not a reference to Satan and his fall as some think. Lucifer is called "this **man** that made the earth to tremble, that did shake the kingdoms" in **14:16**. The king of Babylon is being compared to the morning star, the planet Venus, which brightly appears in the eastern sky just before dawn. But soon it seems to fall from heaven to the earth with the coming of the new day. The glory of the kingdom of Babylon was less than seventy-five years.

---

[21] Don Shackelford, *Truth for Today Commentary, Isaiah.*, p. 181

The Prophecy against Assyria
Isaiah 14:24-27

The LORD of hosts has sworn, saying, "Surely as I have thought, so shall it come to pass; and as I have purposed, so shall it stand: that I will break the Assyrian in my land, and upon my mountains tread him under foot. Then shall his yoke depart from off them, and his burden from off their shoulder." 14:24, 25 What God purposes comes to pass. During the reign of Hezekiah, a good king of Judah, God removed the Assyrian yoke in one night by killing 185,000 Assyrians that were besieging Jerusalem. (Isaiah 37:36-38)

This is the purpose that is purposed upon the whole earth; this is the hand that is stretched out upon all the nations. For the LORD of hosts has purposed, and who can disannul it? 14:26-27 God's removal of Assyria is proof of his power over all the nations. They will rise and fall according to God's thoughts and purposes.

The Prophecy against Philistia
Isaiah 14:28-32

This prophecy came **in the year that king Ahaz died. 14:28** King Ahaz died in 715 BC, and Hezekiah, his son, became king of Judah.

Do not rejoice, all you of Philistia, because the rod that struck you is broken; for out of the serpent's roots will come the viper, and its offspring will be a fiery serpent. 14:29 NKJV The rod is Assyria. When this enemy is broken, Philistia is not to rejoice, because the viper would be Babylon, and the fiery serpent would be Alexander the Great, who would destroy them. (Zechariah 9:5-8)

What shall one then answer the messengers of the nations? That the LORD has founded Zion, and the poor of his people shall trust in it. 14:32 In the last days, the spiritual kingdom of the LORD will be established, and all nations will flow into it, where they will find peace and safety. "For out of Zion shall go forth the law, and the word of the LORD from Jerusalem." (Isaiah 2:2-4)

The Prophecy against Moab
Isaiah 15:1 – 16:14

Moab is laid waste and brought to silence. 15:1 Moab was a small kingdom immediately east of the Dead Sea. The Moabites were descendants of Lot. (Genesis 19:30-37) Balak, king of Moab, hired Balaam to curse Israel in Numbers 22-24. **We have heard the pride of Moab; he is very proud, even of his haughtiness. 16:6** The prophets pronounced judgment on Moab because of her arrogance and idolatry. (Zeph. 2:8-9; Jer. 48:26, 35)

The Prophecy against Syria
Isaiah 17:1-3

Behold, Damascus is taken away from being a city, and it shall be a ruinous heap. 17:1 Damascus was the capital city of Syria. "Damascus is said to be the oldest continuously inhabited city in the world." [22] Homer Hailey explains, "Damascus will cease from being a city of importance; her glory will be as **a ruinous heap**." [23] Immediately after the Assyrian invasion, Damascus may have been left in "a ruinous heap," but because of its location on caravan routes connecting north to south and east to west, it was soon rebuilt by the Assyrians. **The**

---

[22] Don Shackelford, Ibid., p. 204
[23] Homer Hailey, *A Commentary on Isaiah,* p. 153

fortress also shall cease from Ephraim, and the kingdom from Damascus. 17:3 The kingdoms of Israel and Syria were allies against Assyria, and both would be defeated and pass out of existence as nations for a long time.

The Prophecy against Israel
Isaiah 17:4-11

In that day it shall come to pass that the glory of Jacob shall be made thin. 17:4 In the day of Israel's fall in 722 BC, the glory of Jacob (Israel) would be greatly diminished, as of a man made lean by poverty or illness.

At that day a man shall look to his Maker, and his eyes shall have respect to the Holy One of Israel. And he shall not look to the altars, the work of his hands; neither shall respect that which his fingers have made. 17:7-8 In the day of the Lord, the day of judgment, we will recognize God as our Maker and respect Him—and not trust in our own works.

Prophecy against the Invading Nation
Isaiah 17:12-14

Woe to the multitude of many people, which make a noise like the noise of the seas; and to the rushing of nations, that make a rushing like the rushing of mighty waters! The nations shall rush like the rushing of many waters; but God shall rebuke them. 17:12-13 The turbulent "sea" describes ungodly and threatening nations. After the Judgment before the Great White Throne, there shall be "no more sea." (Rev. 20:11-15 and Rev. 21:1) The invading multitude that Isaiah has in mind is the nation of Assyria. **Behold at eveningtide trouble; and before morning he is not. This is the portion of them that spoil us, and the lot of them that rob us. 17:14** King Sennacherib's Assyrian army was a terror in the evening as it besieged Jerusalem, but by morning the Assyrian king was gone. He had returned to his home and remained there at Nineveh. (2 Kings 19:32-37)

The Prophecy against Ethiopia
Isaiah 18

Woe to the land of whirring wings along the rivers of Cush, which sends envoys ... Go, swift messengers, to a people tall and smooth-skinned ... an aggressive nation. ... when a banner is raised on the mountains, you will see it, and when a trumpet sounds, you will hear it. 18:1-3 NIV Cush was the ancient name for Ethiopia, a nation lying south of Egypt. It was a land whirring with insects, but also a land of tall, beautiful, and powerful people. They had sent envoys seeking an alliance with Judah to oppose Assyria. Isaiah is warning Judah against making such an alliance. He tells the Ethiopian "swift messengers" to return to their people and wait for God's trumpet call. At the proper time, God would destroy Assyria.

At that time a present will be brought to the LORD of hosts ... to the place of the name of the LORD of hosts, to Mount Zion. 18:7 NKJV Shackelford says, "Reading this prophecy, one cannot help but think of the Ethiopian official who traveled to Jerusalem to worship seven hundred years later (Acts 8:26-39). He was reading from the scroll of Isaiah the prophet as he was returning home. Phillip, beginning from the passage the official was reading (Is. 53:7, 8), 'preached Jesus to him' (Acts 8:35). The traveler confessed faith in Jesus, was immersed, and went on his way rejoicing (Acts 8:36-39)." [24]

---

[24] Don Shackelford, Ibid., p. 214

The Prophecy against Egypt
Isaiah 19 – 20

Behold, the LORD rides upon a swift cloud, and shall come into Egypt. 19:1 God will cause the Egyptians to fear as he rides on a figurative **cloud** of judgment. They will seek idols, mediums and magicians for help, but find none. Cruel masters and fierce kings will rule over them. **19:2-4** They will suffer from climate change; God will dry up the river Nile, and the brooks will be empty. **19:5-10** Where are the wise men to solve their many problems? **19:11-15** They will be filled with terror and swear allegiance to the LORD. **19:16-18** They will worship and serve the LORD on his spiritual highway and will be united with Israel and Assyria in the LORD's blessing. **19:19-25** This prophecy is fulfilled in Christ and his church. Jesus is the spiritual highway. (John 14:6) All the nations of the earth shall be blessed in Christ. (Galatians 3:8-29)

The Sign against Egypt and Ethiopia
Isaiah 20

In the year that Tartan (title of the commader-in-chief of Assyria's army) **came to Ashdod** to put down a revolt that began in 713 BC, God instructed Isaiah, **"Go, and remove the sackcloth from your body, and take your sandals off your feet." 20:1-2** NKJV For three years, he was to live out God's prophecy by presenting himself in public scantily clothed as a conquered slave, wearing only a short undergarment. In this way, he would to be a sign against Egypt and Ethiopia (Cush) that they would be conquered by the Assyrians. Also, he would serve as a warning to Judah not to make alliances with Egypt and Ethiopia. **20:5-6**

Review Questions on Isaiah 13 – 20

1. What is the meaning of "burden" in Isaiah 13:1?
   _____

2. Was Babylon a world power when Isaiah wrote chapter 13? _____

3. How would the Day of the LORD come? 13:6
   _____

4. God would stir up the _____ against Babylon. 13:17

5. God said Babylon would never be _____ again. 13:19-20

6. Was the destruction of Babylon immediate? _____

7. In Isaiah 14:12, "Lucifer" refers to the _____ of _____.

8. Why was Babylon's glory like the morning star?
   _____

9. The LORD swore, "Surely as I have _____, so shall it come to pass." Isaiah 14:24

10. God said, "I will break the _____ in my land." 14:25

11. Who would destroy Philistia? 14:29
    _____

12. "The LORD has founded _____, and the poor of his people shall trust in it." 14:32

13. Moab was condemned for its _____. 16:6-7

14. Damascus was the capital city of _____. 17:1

15. The glory of _____ would "be made thin." 17:4

16. "At that day, a man shall look to his _____." 17:7

17. "Behold at eveningtide _____, and before the morning he is _____." 17:14

18. Isaiah 17:14 refers to the destruction of the army of king _____ as he besieged Jerusalem.

19. Envoys from _____ were sent to Judah to request an alliance against _____. 18:1

20. A *cloud* figuratively represents _____. 19:1

21. God promised to ____ ____ the rivers and the brooks in Egypt. 19:5-10

22. The Egyptians and the Assyrians would serve the LORD on his spiritual _____. 19:23-25

23. Why was Isaiah scantily clothed for three years? 20:3-6 _____
_____

God Punishes the Nations
Isaiah 21 – 27

The Prophecy of Babylon's Fall
Isaiah 21:1-10

Nebuchadnezzar became king of Babylon in 605 BC, and he made Babylon the most splendid city in the world with its famous Hanging Gardens. Twenty-three years after his death, the Medes and Persians took Babylon without destroying the city in 539 BC.

The burden of the desert of the sea is the title of this prophecy. **21:1** Babylon is in a desert that is watered by the great Euphrates River. **Go up, O Elam! Besiege, O Media! 21:2** Elam is the ancient name for Persia. What an amazing prophecy! Before Babylon became a world power, Isaiah predicted the two nations that would destroy her. Both Persia and Media were east of Babylon, in the area that is now Iran.

Therefore, my loins are filled with pain; pangs have taken hold upon me ... I was bowed down at the hearing of it; I was distressed at the seeing of it. My heart panted, fearfulness frightened me; the night for my pleasure he turned into fear unto me. Prepare the table, watch in the watchtower, eat and drink. Arise, you princes. Anoint the shield. 21:3-5 These verses describe the fears and feelings of Belshazzar, the king of Babylon, on the night of its fall to the Medes and Persians. "His thoughts troubled him ... his knees knocked against each other." NKJV (Dan. 5:6)

"Babylon is fallen, is fallen! And all the graven images of her gods he has broken unto the ground." 21:9

Babylon's idols could not save her. Neither can we save ourselves. Only the LORD God can save us. The shout, "Babylon is fallen, is fallen" is heard in Revelation 14:8 and 18:2 as a repeated warning for us not to trust in the wisdom and power of the world.

The Prophecy against Edom
Isaiah 21:11-12

The burden of Dumah. He calls to me out of Seir ... "Watchman, what of the night?" The watchman said, "The morning comes, and also the night. If ye will inquire, inquire ye. Return, come." 21:11-12 Edom was also called "Seir" after the name of its mountain range. ***Dumah*** is Hebrew for silence. The silence of death would be the judgment for Edom, the land south of the Dead Sea. (Psalms 115:17) Edomites were descendants of Esau (Genesis 25:29-34). They pursued Israel with the sword perpetually and cast off all pity. (Amos 1:11) Edom also aided the Babylonians in the siege and destruction of Jerusalem. They rejoiced when Jerusalem was destroyed and the captives of Judah were taken to Babylon. And like Babylon, Edom would be no more. (Obadiah 1, 10-18) In this vision, someone from Edom was calling the prophet, addressing Isaiah as a watchman. He asks what is left of the night, referring to Assyria's oppression. Edom's present suffering would end as with a new day, but in the future, the end of Edom as nation would come as surely as the night follows the day. The Edomites are encouraged to inquire of the LORD and return to him. They could be part of Messiah's kingdom. (Isaiah 2:2-4)

The Prophecy Against Arabia
Isaiah 21:13-17

In the thickets in Arabia you will lodge, O caravans of Dedanites. To the thirsty bring water; meet the fugitive with bread. O inhabitants of the land of Tema. For they have fled from the swords, from the drawn swords, from the bent bow, and from the press of battle. 21:13-15 ᴱˢⱽ Shackelford observes, "**Dedan** was the son of Abraham by Keturah (1 Chron. 1:32). **Tema** was the son of Ishmael, and the grandson of Abraham (1 Chron. 1:30). Their descendants lived in cities in southern **Arabia** about fifty miles apart. Since Tema was an oasis, it could quench the thirst of the fugitives ... fleeing from invading armies." [25] **The Lord said unto me, "Within a year ... all the glory of Kedar shall fail." 21:16** Kedar was another son of Ishmael. (Genesis 25:13) His descendants inhabited the northern area of Arabia, west of Babylon. The invading armies were probably the Assyrians.

The Prophecy against Jerusalem
Isaiah 22

The burden of the valley of vision. 22:1 The valley of vision is Jerusalem, the holy city of God, who is the source of vision. Although parts of the city are on Mount Moriah and Mount Zion, there are higher mountains surrounding it. To the east is the Mount of Olives. God's judgment against Jerusalem would be the most difficult prophecy for Isaiah to make. This vision describes the decline of Jerusalem, from the siege of the city by the Assyrians in 701 BC to its destruction by the Babylonians in 586 BC.

---

[25] Don Shackelford, Ibid., p. 237

What is the matter with you now, that you have all gone up to the house tops? 22:1 ^{NASB} On the flat roofs of their houses, they could see what was happening and get the news. (Matthew 10:27) Isaiah is using the prophetic perfect tense, by describing future events in the past tense. "God ... calls those things which do not exist as though they did." (Rom. 4:17) ^{NKJV} Isaiah seems to be describing the army of Nebuchadnezzar as it begins the siege of Jerusalem that would end in its destruction. In 701 BC, when Jerusalem was freed from the siege of Sennacherib, the city was full of noise; it was **a tumultuous city, a joyous city. 22:2** Now years later, the Babylonians began a siege of Jerusalem that would last for one year and six months. This time, the outcome would be different.

Isaiah said, "**Your slain were not slain with the sword, nor died in battle." 22.2** They died of starvation and epidemics. (Lamentations 4:4-9) **All your rulers have fled together and have been captured without the bow; all of you who were found were taken captive together, though they had fled far away. 22:3** When Jerusalem fell, Zedekiah king of Judah and all his men fled, but they were captured at Jericho and taken to Nebuchadnezzar, who killed Zedekiah's sons before his eyes. Also, all of the nobles of Judah were killed. They put out Zedekiah's eyes and carried him bound in chains to Babylon. (Jer. 39:1-7)

Isaiah said, "**Look away from me, I will weep bitterly; labor not to comfort me, because of the spoiling of the daughter of my people." 22:4** The prophet refused to be comforted as he saw in a vision the destruction of Jerusalem and the Jews being taken away as captives to Babylon. Archers from the Babylonian province of **Elam** and warriors from nearby **Kir** were involved in this siege of Jerusalem. **22:6**

He has taken away the covering of Judah. 22:8 ᴱˢⱽ The LORD's "covering" had protected Jerusalem earlier, when the Assyrians surrounded their city. But God removed it when the Babylonians came up against Jerusalem and destroyed the city and the temple of God. The LORD had removed his glory from his temple and Jerusalem. (Ezekiel 10:18; 11:23) The people of Jerusalem had looked to armor for their protection, to stones for their fortifications, and to water for their provision. Isaiah said, **"But you did not look to its Maker." 22:8-11** ᴺᴷᴶⱽ There are many who are making the same mistake today. Only the LORD can save us!

And in that day did the Lord GOD of hosts call to weeping and to mourning, to baldness and to girding with sackcloth. 22:12 God was calling for repentance. But instead of repenting, the people of Judah were being fatalistic. They were living a life of self-indulgence and saying, **"Let us eat and drink, for tomorrow we shall die!" 22:13** The Lord responded, **"Surely this iniquity shall not be purged from you till you die." 22:14**

The Prophecy against Shebna
Isaiah 22:15-25

Shebna was the steward of Hezekiah's house. Because he was given to the desire for personal glory, God said, **"I will drive you out of your office." 22:19** Eliakim would replace him, because he would be a faithful servant to God and to the king. (2 Kings 18; Isaiah 36-37) **"The key of the house of David I will lay upon his shoulder; so he shall open, and none shall shut, and he shall shut, and none shall open." 22:22** He would have great authority. (cf. Revelation 3:7)

The Prophecy against Tyre
Isaiah 23

The burden of Tyre. Tyre was the chief city-state of Phoenicia, a country located on the northeast coast of the Mediterranean Sea. The Phoenicians were skilled sailors, and they established colonies in North Africa, Spain, and Sicily. They became very wealthy merchants. Hiram king of Tyre was a friend to David and Solomon, and he provided the cedar and cypress for Solomon's palace and the Lord's temple. (1 Kings 5:8-10) However, the Phoenicians also had a bad influence on Israel. Solomon married women of Phoenicia, who influenced him to worship Ashtoreth, the goddess of the Sidonians. (1 Kings 11:1, 5)

Howl, you ships of Tarshish; for it is laid waste, so that there is no house, no entering in. 23:1 Tyre was not laid waste in the days of Isaiah. Over a hundred years later, the prophet Ezekiel was still predicting its fall. "In their wailing for you they will take up a lamentation, and lament for you: 'What city is like Tyre, destroyed in the midst of the sea?'" (Ezekiel 27:32) ^{NKJV} The island city of Tyre was destroyed by Alexander the Great in 332 BC. [26] Spanish ships from Tarshish could not find in Tyre a harbor or housing for sailors.

Tyre shall be forgotten seventy years ... And it shall come to pass after the end of seventy years that the LORD will visit Tyre, and she shall turn to her hire. 23:15, 17 The Phoenicians became a rival of Rome after the city of Tyre was rebuilt. Their most prosperous colony was Carthage in North Africa. The first of three wars between Carthage and Rome broke out in 264 BC. At the end of third war, Carthage was destroyed by the Romans, never to be rebuilt. The glory of Tyre was gone with the fall of Carthage in 149 BC.

---

[26] Louis L. Orlin, *The World Book Encyclopedia*, 1974 Edition, Vol. 19, p. 445

The LORD of hosts has purposed it, to stain the pride of all glory. 23:9 God dishonors the pride of man. Don Shackelford makes this observation, "The oracle against Tyre was likely placed here to bracket this series of oracles. Like Babylon in the east, Tyre in the west summed up all that the world thought to be significant. The pride of both led to their downfall." [27]

The Judgment of the Earth
Isaiah 24

Behold, the LORD makes the earth empty and makes it waste ... and scatters abroad the inhabitants. 24:1 The judgments in chapters 13-23 prefigure the final Judgment Day. The messages of warning and of hope in chapters 24-27 are for the whole world. God's wrath may be seen during our present time, "For the wrath of God is revealed from heaven against all ungodliness and unrighteousness of men." (Rom. 1:18) The Bible also speaks about "the day of wrath and the revelation of the righteous judgment of God" at the end of time. (Rom. 2:5) When Christ returns, he will raise all the dead (John 5:28) and **empty the earth** of all its inhabitants, as they are caught up to his judgment seat. (2 Cor. 5:10) Some will hear him say, "Come, you blessed of my Father," and others will hear, "Depart from me, you cursed." (Matthew 25:31-34, 41) There will be a great **scattering**, some to heaven and others to hell. When the final "day of the Lord" comes "the heavens shall pass away with a great noise, and the elements shall melt with fervent heat, the earth also and the works that are therein shall be burned up." (2 Pet. 3:10) God will **make the earth waste.**

---

[27] Don Shackelford, Ibid., p. 254

And it shall be: as with the people, so with the priest; as with the servant, so with his master. 24:2 On the last day of God's wrath, he "will render to each one according to his deeds …for there is no partiality with God." (Romans 2:6,11) ᴺᴷᴶⱽ

The earth also is defiled under its inhabitants because they have transgressed the laws, changed the ordinance, broken the everlasting covenant. Therefore, the curse has devoured the earth, and they that dwell there are desolate. Therefore, the inhabitants of the earth are burned, and few men are left. 24:5-6 After God had created the heaven and the earth, he "saw everything that he had made, and behold, it was very good." (Genesis 1:31) But man has defiled the earth by transgressing God's laws. After the flood, God made an **everlasting covenant** with all mankind (Genesis 9:16), in which the shedding of innocent blood was forbidden. (Genesis 9:5-6) Therefore, the earth is cursed and will be destroyed. We are reminded that **few men are left**; only a remnant will be saved. Jesus said, "Because strait is the gate and narrow is the way that leads unto life, and **few** there be that find it." (Matthew 7:14)

In the city is left desolation, and the gate is smitten with destruction. 24:7-12 Prior to the final judgment, God punishes individuals and nations with wars, droughts, famines, epidemics, and failed economies. We have seen these sufferings in the prophecies made against the nations in chapters 13-23.

When thus it shall be in the midst of the land among the people, in the midst of human suffering, the righteous remnant will praise the LORD. **They shall lift up their voice, they shall sing; for the majesty of the LORD. 24:13, 14**

But Isaiah said, **"Woe unto me! The treacherous dealers have dealt treacherously." 24:16** Isaiah was suffering because of sinners. Jesus said, "In the world you shall have tribulation; but be of good cheer, I have overcome the world." (John 16:33)

The earth is violently broken, the earth is split open, the earth is shaken exceedingly. The earth shall reel to and fro like a drunkard, and shall totter like a hut; its transgression shall be heavy upon it, and it will fall, and not rise again." 24:19-20 NJKV This description of God's judgment upon the earth is like the pouring out of the seventh bowl of God's wrath in Revelation 16:17-20. The earth will be no more. In 1 John 2:17, we are reminded, "the world is passing away, and the lusts of it; but he who does the will of God abides forever." NKJV

It shall come to pass in that day, that the LORD shall punish the host of the high ones that are on high, and the kings of the earth upon the earth. 24:21 In the day that the earth is broken up and falls, not to rise again (vv. 19-20), the LORD will punish **the host of exalted ones**, "the spiritual host of wickedness in heavenly places." (Ephesians 6:12) The angels who sinned are "reserved in everlasting chains under darkness for the judgment of the great day." (Jude 6) God will also punish the wicked kings of the earth. (Revelation 19:19-21)

The moon and the sun shall be no more **when the LORD of hosts shall reign on Mount Zion and in Jerusalem. 24:23** The Lord God omnipotent will reign on his throne on Mount Zion in heaven (Revelation 19:6) and in the heavenly New Jerusalem. (Revelation 21:1 – 22:5)

God's Judgments, Salvation, and Victory
Isaiah 25 – 27

O LORD, you are my God; I will exalt you, I will praise your name, for you have done wonderful things; your counsels of old are faithfulness and truth. 25:1 The LORD has done wonderful things! God's plans from the beginning have been faithfully performed in truth. God has destroyed the power and the pride of men along with their fortified cities and palaces. God has provided for the poor and has protected the needy. **And in this mountain the LORD of hosts shall make unto all people a feast. 25:6** God reigns on his throne in heavenly Mount Zion. (Rev. 14:1-3) A great multitude from all nations will praise God for their salvation, and there will be a great feast in heaven. (Rev. 19:6-9) **And he will destroy in this mountain the face of the covering cast over all people, and the veil that is spread over all nations. 25:7** Isaiah will write, "Behold, the darkness shall cover the earth, and gross darkness the people; but the LORD shall arise upon you and his glory shall be seen upon you. And the Gentiles shall come to your light." (62:2-3) The apostle Paul wrote that Christ has "brought life and immorality to light through the gospel." (2 Timothy 1:10) When one turns to the Lord, "the veil is taken away," according to 2 Corinthians 3:16.

He will swallow up death in victory, and the Lord GOD will wipe away tears from off all faces. 25:8 The first part of this verse is mentioned in 1 Corinthians 15:54; and the second part is fulfilled in Revelation 7:17 and 21:4.

And it shall be said in that day, "Lo, this is our God; we have waited for him, and he will save us. This is the LORD; we have waited for him, we will be glad and rejoice in his salvation. For in this mountain the hand of the LORD shall rest, and Moab shall be trodden down under him." 25:9-10 Moab symbolizes all the sinful nations of the world. Moab was a constant enemy of Israel from the time of the exodus. Balak king of Moab hired the prophet Balaam to curse Israel, but God turned each attempt to curse into a blessing for Israel. However, Balaam advised Balak to invite the Israelites to the sacrifices to Moab's gods and to commit harlotry with the women of Moab. Then the LORD cursed Israel by killing 24,000 of their men with a plague. (Num. 22 – 25) Christians may be tempted to follow "the doctrine of Balaam" (Revelation 2:14), but God's faithful servants will patiently wait for the salvation from the LORD. They will be glad that they did, and they will rejoice.

"You will keep him in perfect peace whose mind is stayed on you, because he trusts in you." 26:3

With my soul I have desired you in the night; yes, with my spirit within me I will seek you early. For when your judgments are in the earth, the inhabitants of the world will learn righteousness. 26:9

LORD, in trouble they have visited you, they poured out a prayer when your chastening was upon them. 26:16 The trials we suffer while here on earth should cause us to repent and return to God.

Your dead shall live; together with my dead body they shall rise. Awake and sing, you who dwell in dust; for your dew is like the dew of herbs, and the earth shall cast out the dead. 26:19 ^{NKJV} The resurrection of the dead is coming. (John 5:28-29)

Behold, the LORD **comes out of his place to punish the inhabitants of the earth for their iniquity. 26:21**

In that day the LORD **will punish Leviathan, the fleeting serpent, with His fierce and great and mighty sword, even Leviathan the twisted serpent; and He will kill the dragon who lives in the sea. 27:1** ^NASB Satan is "the dragon, that serpent of old" in Revelation 20:2. The **sea** is a symbol for the ungodly nations. [28] The LORD will use his spiritual sword, His word (Hebrews 4:12), to destroy the devil. (Rev. 20:10) Satan is described in several ways. He is called **a fleeting serpent** because his time is relatively short (Rev. 12:12), **a twisted serpent** because he has been twisting God's truth from the beginning (Genesis 3:1-5, John 8: 44), and **the dragon** because of his destructive power (Rev. 9:11).

In that day— **"Sing about a fruitful vineyard: I, the L**ORD**, watch over it; I water it continually. I guard it day and night so that no one may harm it," 27:2-3** ^NIV In chapter 5, Isaiah used an unfruitful vineyard to describe Israel. The nation was unfaithful to God and failed to produce good fruit. The faithful remnant is God's fruitful vineyard. **He shall cause those that come of Jacob to take root; Israel shall blossom and bud and fill the face of the world with fruit. 27:6** The first vineyard was physical Israel; the new vineyard is spiritual Israel. Jesus Christ is the true vine and his disciples are the fruitful branches. (John 15:1-8)

Has the LORD **struck her as he struck those who struck her? Has she been killed as those were killed who killed her? 27:7** ^NIV The LORD has punished Israel for her sins but not as He punished Assyria and Babylon. They would be no more. A remnant of Israel, spiritual Israel would be saved.

---

[28] Revelation 17:1, 15; Revelation 13:1-7, Isaiah 17:12-13

Therefore by this, the guilt of Jacob will be atoned for, and this will be the full fruit of the removal of his sin: when he makes all the stones of the altars like chalkstones crushed to pieces, no Asherim or incense altars will remain standing. 27:9 ^{ESV} Israel must reject every form of idolatry. Forgiveness of sin is conditional; genuine repentance is necessary. It will lead to godly living. We are to "bear fruit in keeping with repentance." ^{ESV} (Matthew 3:8)

Yet the defenced city shall be desolate, and the habitation forsaken. 27:10 ^{KJV} The cities of Israel were destroyed; and its people were exiled. The majority of physical Israel was **a people of no understanding.**

Therefore, he that made them will not have mercy on them. 27:11 God had made Israel a nation, but it had become like the other nations, and because they refused to repent, God would destroy Jerusalem in 586 BC and again in AD 70. The LORD's mercy is upon the few of all nations that trust and obey him. They are not seeking the passing pleasures and riches of this world. Their desire is a relationship with God and the eternal blessings of heaven. Standing in the midst of the destruction of Jerusalem, Jeremiah could say, "The steadfast love of the LORD never ceases, his mercies never come to an end, they are new every morning; great is your faithfulness. 'The LORD is my portion,' says my soul, therefore I will hope in him." (Lamentations 3:22-24) ^{ESV} God's people have been called out of darkness into his marvelous light. (1 Peter 2:9-10) Spiritual Israel is the true Israel, the redeemed from all nations. (Galatians 6:14-16)

And it will come about in that day, that the LORD will start *His* threshing from the flowing streams of the Euphrates to the brook of Egypt; and you will be gathered one by one, O sons of Israel. 27:12 ^{NASB} God promised this land to Abraham's descendants in

Genesis 15:18. Homer Hailey says, "However, we are not to think of a literal area but should regard the phrase as symbolic of the world over which God rules." [29] "In that day" refers to the Christian Age. Threshing represents judging. A farmer threshes the wheat to separate the grain from the chaff. He gathers the grain and destroys the chaff. God separates the believers from the unbelievers by the preaching of the gospel. (Mark 16:15-16) This prophecy is fulfilled in the church, where individuals are gathered **one by one.** (Acts 2:47) Christians have been sanctified, set apart from the world, in order to serve the Lord. God will judge his people; we will not be judged as a group or as a nation, but individually. Eternal promises are made to the individual that "overcomes" in Revelation 2:7; 2:11; 2:17; 2:26-29; 3:5-6; 3:12-13; and 3:21-22.

It will come about also in that day that a great trumpet will be blown; and those who were perishing in the land of Assyria and who were scattered in the land of Egypt will come and worship the LORD in the holy mountain at Jerusalem. 27:13 [NASB] Hailey says, "The sounding of this trumpet might be both a call to assemble on the mountain for worship and an announcement that atonement for sin has been perfectly provided in the sacrifice to which the law points. The idolatry of Jacob has been expiated, that is, removed from God's view (v. 9); atonement for sin has been made. The outcasts from the two extremes (as in v. 12), from Assyria to Egypt, are now being called that they might *worship Jehovah in the holy mountain at Jerusalem* (cf. 24:23; 25:6-7, 10). The writer of Hebrews says it is to this mountain, the heavenly Jerusalem, and to the blood of Jesus we have now come." [30] Those of Israel that were perishing among nations because of Assyria and the poor

---

[29] Homer Hailey, Ibid., p. 223
[30] Homer Hailey, Ibid., p. 224

Jews that were in the land of Egypt were able to return to Jerusalem and rebuild the temple by the decree of Cyrus in 536 BC. (Ezra 1:1-4) This gathering foreshadowed the Day of Pentecost in Acts 2, when those of all nations heard the gospel of salvation preached for the first time. "You are come unto Mount Zion, and unto the city of the living God, the heavenly Jerusalem." (Hebrews 12:22)

Review Questions on Isaiah 21 – 27

1. _____ and _____ will besiege Babylon. 21:2

2. The feelings of King _____ on the night that his kingdom fell are described in Isaiah 21:3-5.

3. "_____ is fallen, is fallen!" 21:9

4. The _____, descendants of Esau, are denounced for fighting against _____.

5. Isaiah 21:13-17 is a prophecy against _____.

6. The inhabitants of Jerusalem did not realize that God had removed the _____ of Judah. 22:8

7. They looked to armor, stones, and water for their protection, but they "did not look to its _____." 22:8-11

8. The people said, "Let us _____ and _____, for tomorrow we shall _____." 22:13

9. Who replaced Shebna as the steward of the king's house? 22:15-22 _____

10. Isaiah 22:22 is applied to _____ in Revelation 3:7.

11. Isaiah 23 is the prophecy against _____, the chief city-state of _____.

12. "Behold, the LORD makes the earth _____ and makes it _____." 24:1

13. The remnant "shall lift up their _____, they shall _____ for the _____ of the LORD." 24:14

14. The LORD will _____ on Mount Zion. 24:23

15. "I will praise your name, for you have done _____ things." 25:1

16. "He will swallow up _____ in victory."

17. "And the Lord GOD will wipe away _____ from off all faces." 25:8

18. "You will keep him in perfect peace, whose _____ is stayed on You." 26:3

19. Why is Satan called a **fleeting, twisted** serpent? 27:1 _____
    _____

20. Israel would be gathered _____ by _____. 27:12

NOTES

Woes and Blessings
Isaiah 28 – 35

Woe to the crown of pride, to the drunkards of Ephraim. 28:1 Disaster and doom were coming to the nation of Israel. Like the fading beauty of a flower, their glory was vanishing. Israel's proud kings and leaders were thinking and behaving as drunkards. They were being confused by strong drink. Hosea said of them, "They have deserted the LORD to give themselves to prostitution, to old wine and new, which take way the understanding of my people." (Hosea 4:11) ^{NIV}

Behold, the LORD has a mighty and strong one. 28:2 The crown of pride, the drunkards of Ephraim, shall be trodden under foot. 28:3 God would use the Assyrians to destroy the nation of Israel. The Assyrians would be like a destroying storm, a flood of overflowing mighty waters. The date of this prophecy was before the fall of the northern kingdom of Israel in 722 BC.

In that day the LORD of hosts shall be for a crown of glory and for a diadem of beauty unto the remnant of his people. 28:5 "In that day" refers to the destruction of the kingdom of Israel. "The remnant of his people" would be Jerusalem and the kingdom of Judah. **But they also have erred through wine. 28:7** The kingdom of Judah under king Ahaz also had been unfaithful, but the LORD in his mercy would be their "crown of glory."

The priest and the prophet have erred through strong drink; they are swallowed up of wine, they are out of the way through strong drink. 28:7 The priests and the prophets were among Jerusalem's scornful rulers. (v. 14) The priests were not to drink wine or intoxicating drink so they might be able to "teach the children of Israel all the statues which the LORD had spoken unto them by the hand of Moses." (Lev. 10:8-11) But how could the LORD teach through drunken priests? These scornful were treating God's faithful prophet Isaiah with derision. They scoffed, **"Whom shall he teach knowledge? And whom shall he make to understand doctrine? Them that are weaned from the milk? 28:9** He teaches us like little children, saying, **'For precept must be upon precept, precept upon precept; line upon line, line upon line, here a little, and there a little.'" 28:10** The simplicity of God's way of teaching offends the pride of sinners.

For with stammering lips and another tongue he will speak to this people. To whom he said, "This is the rest wherewith you may cause the weary to rest; and this is the refreshing." Yet they would not hear. 28:11-12 God was sending the Assyrians, men of another tongue, to teach Judah to respect the warnings of the LORD by destroying all the fortified cities of Judah. (2 Kings 18:13) God's destruction of the Assyrian army that was besieging Jerusalem was **the rest** that caused the weary to rest, and this was the refreshing. But after king Hezekiah died, the people returned to their sinful ways; "they would not hear."

Because the drunken prophets and priests ridiculed **the word of the LORD** as being simple **precept upon precept, precept upon precept; line upon line, line upon line,** they would **fall backward and be broken, and snared and taken. 28:13** In 586 BC, Jerusalem would be destroyed, and its people would be taken to Babylon. Hailey notes, "A remnant did eventually learn, but it was precept upon precept, line upon line, little by little."[31] Many need to learn this lesson today. We are to "receive with meekness" God's word. (James 1:21)

---

[31] Homer Hailey, *A Commentary on Isaiah*, p. 231

Isaiah pleaded, **"Hear the word of the Lord, you scornful men that rule this people which is in Jerusalem." 28:14** The king's political advisors were scoffing at the warnings of the Lord, because they had made an alliance with Egypt for their protection. Isaiah expresses sarcastically their attitude with these words: **"We have made a covenant with death, and with hell we are at agreement. When the overflowing scourge shall pass through, it shall not come to us, for we have made lies our refuge, and under falsehood we hid ourselves." 28:15**

Therefore, thus says the Lord God, "Behold, I lay in Zion for a foundation a stone, a tried stone, a precious cornerstone, a sure foundation; he that believes shall not make haste." 28:16 In response to those trusting in alliances with other nations, God reveals the sure foundation of faith. Shackelford says, "For the people of Isaiah's time, surely the Lord's promise of deliverance was the rock of their faith. However, the precious cornerstone would ultimately be realized in Jesus Christ. In fact, Peter quoted this verse, applying it to Jesus (1 Peter 2:6). Paul said that the church is 'built on the foundation of the apostles and prophets, Christ Jesus Himself being the chief cornerstone' (Ephesians 2:20). Paul referred to this verse twice (Romans 9:33; Romans 10:11) to indicate that Jesus is the cornerstone upon which Christians must build their faith." [32]

"I will make justice the measuring line and righteousness the level; the hail will sweep away the refuge of lies and the waters will overflow the secret place. Your covenant with death will be canceled." 28:17 NASB God's judgments would destroy their trust in lies and in their alliances with other nations.

---

[32] Don Shackelford, *Truth for Today Commentary, Isaiah,* p. 297

"For the bed is shorter than that a man can stretch himself on it; and the covering narrower than that he can wrap himself in it." 28:20 "The rulers of Judah will find their covenant and agreement of lies too short and too narrow for protection." [33]

Woe to Ariel, to Ariel, the city where David dwelt! 29:1 "Ariel" refers to Jerusalem, the city of David. The word originally meant "lion of God," but it is translated "altar" in Ezekiel 43:15. Since the annual feasts also are mentioned in Isaiah 29:1, the "altar" seems to be the meaning that would describe Jerusalem where sacrifices were made in God's temple.

And I will camp against you round about and will lay siege against you. 29:3 Jerusalem was first besieged by the Assyrians. The second siege lasted one year, and six months; and then the Babylonians destroyed both the city and the temple. (2 Kings 25:1-9) The fall of Jerusalem would seem like a nightmare. **29:4-8**

They are drunken, but not with wine; they stagger, but not with strong drink. 29:9 The leaders of Judah were spiritually drunk. They were not thinking or seeing clearly; they were out of control in their actions.

For the LORD has poured out upon you the spirit of deep sleep and has closed your eyes. 29:10 Homer Hailey explains, "This means that when we reject God and His truth, God has no alternative but to give us up to error and evil."[34] God gives unbelievers "over to a reprobate mind" (Romans 1:28), so "that they should believe a lie." (2 Thess. 2:10-12)

---

[33] Homer Hailey, Ibid., p. 234
[34] Homer Hailey, Ibid., p. 243

The LORD said, "**This people draw near me with their mouth and with their lips do honor me, but have removed their heart far from me, and their fear toward me is taught by the precept of men. Therefore, behold, I will proceed to do a marvelous work among this people, even a marvelous work and a wonder: for the wisdom of their wise men shall perish, and the understanding of their prudent men shall be hid." 29:13-14** Their worship was hypocritical and not from the heart. It was merely a routine. Jesus used this passage to expose the vain worship of the scribes and Pharisees in his day. (Matthew 15:8-9) Paul referred to the last part of verse 14 in 1 Corinthians 1:19, "I will destroy the wisdom of the wise, and bring to nothing the understanding of the prudent."

Woe unto them that seek deep to hide their counsel from the LORD, and their works are in the dark. And they say, "Who sees us?" and, "Who knows us?" 29:15 Those who think they can conceal their actions and thoughts from God are practicing a type of atheism. "All things are naked and opened unto the eyes of Him with whom we have to do." (Hebrews 4:13)

Shall the potter be esteemed as the clay; for shall the thing made say of him who made it, "He did not make me"? Or shall the thing formed say of him who formed it, "He has no understanding"? 29:16[NKJV] Shackelford says, "**The potter** is a reference to God. Isaiah showed how ridiculous it would be to consider **clay** as being equal to the potter ... Paul used the same imagery of the potter to answer those who charge God falsely for His actions of wrath against evildoers and mercy to those who obey Him. He has made His mercy available to both Jews and Gentiles (Romans 9:19-24)." [35]

---

[35] Don Shackelford, Ibid., p. 307-308

Is it not a yet a very little while, and Lebanon (well-known for its forest) **shall be turned into a fruitful field. And the fruitful field shall be esteemed as a forest? 29:17** God turns things around! God makes the changes!

In that day the deaf shall hear the words of the book, and the eyes of the blind shall see out of obscurity and out of darkness. The meek also shall increase their joy in the LORD; and the poor among men shall rejoice in the Holy One of Israel. 29:18-19 The people had been spiritually deaf and blind. But with the coming of Christ, the humble would rejoice in the Lord because they could understand the word of God and perceive those things that had been obscure.

Therefore, thus says the LORD, who redeemed Abraham concerning the house of Jacob, "Jacob shall not now be ashamed, neither shall his face now wax pale. But when he sees his children, the work of my hands, in the midst of him, they will sanctify my name, and sanctify the Holy One of Jacob, and shall fear the God of Israel." 29:22-23 Physical Israel's disobedience had caused Jacob to be ashamed, but now he sees the remnant, his spiritual children, making the name of the LORD holy, and they are reverencing God. Peter exhorted, "Sanctify Christ as Lord in your hearts, always being ready to make a defense to everyone who asks you to give a reason for the hope that is in you, yet with gentleness and reverence." NASB (1 Pet. 3:15)

"They also that erred in spirit shall come to understanding, and they that murmured shall learn doctrine." 29:24 Some who had complained about the simplicity of God's word would come to understanding. Christ's gospel is God's power to save us. (Rom. 1:16) The message of the cross is not foolishness; it has the power to change hearts. (1 Cor. 1:18-31)

"**Woe to the rebellious children,**" says the L<small>ORD</small>, "**That take counsel, but not of me ... that they may add sin to sin; that walk to go down into Egypt and have not asked at my mouth.**" **30:1-2** Shackelford explains, "The rulers of Judah...were determined to **make an alliance** with Egypt. In face of danger they were willfully trusting in human intervention (that is, in help from Egypt) rather than relying on God's help. To misplace our faith is **to sin**." [36]

This is a rebellious people...children that will not hear the law of the of the L<small>ORD</small>; which say to the seers, "See not," and to the prophets, "Prophesy not unto us right things; speak unto us smooth things, prophesy deceits." **30:9-10** Paul also warns of such people in 2 Timothy 4:2-4.

For thus says the Lord G<small>OD</small>, the Holy One of Israel: "In returning and rest you shall be saved; in quietness and confidence shall be your strength." **30:15** Salvation requires repentance. In returning to the L<small>ORD</small>, they would be saved from their enemies and find rest. Faith in God is our strength that produces calmness and confidence.

But you said, "No!" **30:16** In refusing God and his salvation, they would have to flee and be overtaken by their enemies. They would be a negative example of all those that reject God. **30:17**

And therefore, the L<small>ORD</small> will wait, that he may be gracious unto you, and therefore he will be exalted, that he may have mercy upon you. Blessed are all they that wait for him. 30:18 God patiently waits for sinners of Judah to realize the consequences of rejecting him. "The Lord is longsuffering to us, not willing that any should

---

[36] Don Shackelford, Ibid., p. 313

perish, but that all should come to repentance." (2 Peter 3:9) He will be exalted in his mercy and grace. Those that patiently wait for God during difficult and trying times will be blessed like the prophet Isaiah and King Hezekiah.

For the people shall dwell in Zion at Jerusalem. You shall weep no more. He will be very gracious unto you at the voice of your cry; when he shall hear it, he will answer you. 30:19 God answered the prayer of King Hezekiah when Jerusalem was besieged. (37:15-23; 36-38) Jerusalem was spared, and its people wept no more. This event foreshadows the salvation of all who wait for the Lord. They shall dwell in heavenly Zion as the New Jerusalem, where "God shall wipe away all tears." (Rev. 21:1-4)

And though the Lord give you the bread of adversity and the water of affliction, yet your teachers shall not be removed into a corner any more, but your eyes shall see your teachers. 30:20 They had put God's prophets in "a corner" and had refused to hear God's word (verses 9-10). But after suffering the Assyrians' siege of Jerusalem, they would desire to hear God's prophets and follow their directions. They would cast their idols away as an unclean thing. God would bless them with rain and fruitful crops and cattle, and their nation would be restored. **30:21-26**

Behold, the name of the Lord **comes from far. 30:27 For through the voice of the** Lord**, the Assyrian shall be beaten down, which smote with a rod. 30:31** Assyria's defeat is described in verses 27-33.

For Topheth has long been ready. Indeed, it has been prepared for the king. He has made it deep and large, a pyre of fire with plenty of wood; the breath of the Lord

like a torrent of brimstone sets it afire. 30:33 ^NASB^ Hailey says, "Such a place has long been provided for both kings and nations like Assyria. *Topheth* is the site in the Valley of Hinnom where children had been burned as offerings to Molech, a custom of the Canaanites which apostates of Judah adopted (II Kings 23:10). The New Testament word *Gehenna*, the place of eternal burning, is derived from the Hebrew 'Valley of Hinnom.'" [37]

Woe to them that go down to Egypt for help ... but they look not unto the Holy One of Israel, neither seek the LORD! 31:1 God is more powerful than men, horses, and chariots. **Like as the lion and the young lion roaring on his prey ... so the LORD of hosts shall come down to fight for mount Zion. 31:4** The LORD will protect Zion and Jerusalem from the Assyrians.

Turn to him from whom the children of Israel have deeply revolted. For in that day every man shall cast away his idols. 31:6, 7 During the days of Ahaz king of Judah, the people had turned from the LORD to idols. Ahaz "made molded images of the Baals. He burned incense in the Valley of the Son of Hinnom and burned his children in the fire according to the abominations of the nations." And he "shut up the doors of the house of God and made for himself altars in every corner of Jerusalem. And in every single city of Judah he made high places to burn incense to other gods and provoked to anger the LORD." ^NKJV^ (2 Chron 28:2-3, 24-25) However, when his son became king of Judah, things changed for the better. Hezekiah "did that which was right in the sight of the LORD. He in the first year of his reign, in the first month, opened the doors of the house of the LORD and repaired them." (2 Chronicles 29:1-3) All the images of pagan gods and their altars were destroyed in all the cities of Judah. (2 Chronicles 31:1)

---

[37] Homer Hailey, Ibid., p. 262

Then shall the Assyrian fall with the sword, not of a mighty man. 31:8 This was fulfilled in 701 BC when "the angel of the LORD went out and killed in the camp of the Assyrians one hundred and eighty-five thousand. So, Sennacherib king of Assyria departed." (2 Kings 19:35, 36) NKJV The Assyrian kingdom came to an end in 612 BC when the Babylonians laid waste Nineveh, their capital city. The LORD had determined their end, as revealed by his prophet Nahum. (Nahum 3:5-6) God said, "I shall put my sword into the hand of the king of Babylon, and he shall stretch it out upon the land of Egypt." (Ezekiel 20:24-25) In like manner, the LORD also put his sword in the hand of Babylon to destroy Assyria. God causes nations to fall.

Behold a king will reign in righteousness and his princes shall rule in judgment. 32:1 Hezekiah was a king who reigned in righteousness, and his nation was saved. He serves as a type of the messianic king, Jesus Christ, by whose righteousness we are saved. Christians are described as a "royal priesthood" in 1 Peter 2:9, and they are the princes that rule with justice. (cf. Rev. 5:10)

And a man shall be as a hiding place from the wind, and a covert from the tempest. 32:2 King Hezekiah, Isaiah, and all those who put their trust in God were the refuge of hope when the Assyrians came up against Jerusalem and besieged it. (2 Kings 19:1-19) Today, the followers of Christ are a protective influence and a refuge of hope in the world. (Matthew 5:13-16)

Then the eyes of those who see will not be blinded, and the ears of those who hear will listen. The mind of the hasty will discern the truth, and the tongue of the stammerers will hasten to speak clearly. 32:3-4 NASB Christ gives spiritual sight, hearing, understanding, and the ability to communicate the truth. (Eph. 1:18; 4:15, 21)

No longer will the fool be called noble, nor the scoundrel be highly respected. 32:5 ^{NIV} One who rejects God is a fool, although the world may praise and honor him. Believers will show no respect for fools, for a fool speaks nonsense and a scoundrel devises wicked schemes. **32:6-7 But the noble man makes noble plans, and by noble deeds he stands. 32:8** ^{NIV}

Rise up you women who are at ease and hear my voice; give ear to my word, you complacent daughters. Within a year and a few days, you will be troubled, O complacent daughters; for the vintage is ended, and the fruit gathering will not come. 32:9-10 ^{NASB} Isaiah speaks to the women, because of their great influence upon men and children. They are responsible for providing food for their families. The women had not been listening to the prophet's warnings, because they were over-confident and indifferent. God soon would begin his judgment against his ungodly nation. The Assyrian army would conquer all their fortified cities. (2 Kings 18:13) When Jerusalem is besieged, food would become scarce. The prophet instructs the women to put on sackcloth, a sign of repentance. **32:11**

The devastation caused by sins will last **until the Spirit is poured upon us from on high and the wilderness is a fruitful field. 32:15** The Spirit was poured out when the angel of the LORD destroyed the 185,000 soldiers of the Assyrian army, and Jerusalem was spared. (2 Kings 19:35-37) The Jews were exiled in Babylon, until God's Spirit stirred up the spirit of Cyrus king of Persia and he decreed that they could return to their homeland and rebuild Jerusalem and the temple. (Ezra 1:1-4; Isaiah 44:28) The ultimate fulfillment came on the day of Pentecost, when the Holy Spirit was poured on the apostles to reveal the gospel of Christ. (Acts 2:1-4, 16-21)

The work of righteousness shall be peace; and the effect of righteousness quietness and assurance forever. 32:17 Christ is our peace (Ephesians 2:14-17); for he is "the Prince of Peace." (Isaiah 9:6)

Woe to you who plunder, though you have not been plundered; and you who deal treacherously, though they have not dealt treacherously with you! 33:1 Sennacherib king of Assyria plundered Judah and dealt treacherously with Hezekiah king of Judah. After Sennacherib had received a payment of tribute from Hezekiah, he then came up against Jerusalem. (2 Kings 18:14-17)

O Lord, be gracious unto us; we have waited for you; be our salvation also in the time of trouble. 33:2 This was Hezekiah's prayer when Jerusalem was besieged by the Assyrians. (2 Kings 19:15-19)

The Lord is exalted, for he dwells on high; he has filled Zion with justice and righteousness. The fear of the Lord is his treasure. 33:5, 6 Verses 7-9 describe the conditions at the time of the siege. Brave men were crying publicly, ambassadors of peace wept because the Assyrians had broken their covenant, the highways were deserted of travelers, and the land had become like a wilderness. But there was a faithful remnant in Zion that feared the Lord.

Then the Lord said, **"Now I will rise; now I will be exalted; now I will lift up myself." 33:10** God's judgment upon the Assyrians is described as burning the chaff and stubble with fire in **verses 11-12**.

"Hear you that are far off, what I have done; and you that are near, acknowledge my might." 33:13 God wanted both the Gentiles and the Jews to recognize his power in destroying the Assyrian army by his angel in one night. After witnessing God's mighty power, **the sinners in Zion are terrified; trembling has seized the godless. 33:14** ^(NASB) On Judgment Day, both the impenitent sinners among God's people and those that reject God will be filled with fear.

He that walks righteously, and speaks uprightly, he that despises the gain of oppressions, that shakes his hands from holding of bribes, that stops his ears from hearing of bloodshed, and shuts his eyes from seeing evil, he shall dwell on high ... Your eyes shall see the King in his beauty; they shall behold the land that is very far off. 33:15-17 The righteous shall dwell on high and see God the King in his beauty in the land very far away. What a wonderful description of heaven! **For the LORD is our judge, the LORD is our lawgiver, the LORD is our king; he will save us. 33:22 The people that dwell therein shall be forgiven their iniquity. 33:24**

Come near, ye nations, to hear; and listen, ye people! For the indignation of the LORD is upon all nations, and his fury upon all their armies; he has utterly destroyed them, he has delivered them to the slaughter ... All the host of heaven shall be dissolved, and the heavens shall be rolled together as a scroll; and all their host shall fall down as the leaf falls from the vine, and as a falling fig from the fig tree. 34:1-4 God's days of judgment against nations may be clearly seen in history; nations are destroyed by the mighty hand of God. Hailey states, "Although the picture portrayed in these verses may foreshadow the end of the world, the prophet does not have this in mind. Rather, he is describing in strong metaphor the end of the world for the heathen nations. When God's wrath and indignation come against the nations that oppose and fight Him, their world comes to an end." [38] Don Shackelford adds, "Both

---

[38] Homer Hailey, Ibid., p. 288

Matthew 24:29 and Revelation 6:13, 14 echo the imagery of verse 4 in describing changes wrought in the earth by God's judgment." [39] God's judgment of wicked nations is under the sixth seal in Revelation 6:13-14. The final Day of Judgment at the end of the world is under the seventh seal in Revelation 11:15-18.

For my sword shall be bathed in heaven; behold, it shall come down on Edom, and on the people of my curse, to judgment. 34:5 Don Shackelford explains, "Edom, or Idumea, is singled out in chapter 34 as representative of the nations who were hostile to God and His people. Edom entered into the biblical account in the person of Esau, Jacob's brother. As there was enmity between these sons of Isaac, so there was between their descendants. Throughout the national life of the Jews under the kings, Edom was an enemy (1 Kings 11:14). The Edomites delighted in the destruction of Jerusalem (Ps. 137:7). The prophets noted Edom's violence (Joel 3:19; Amos 1:11, 12) and spoke of Edom's destruction (Jer. 49:7-22; Ezek. 25:12-14; see Obad. 8; Mal. 1:4)." [40] Isaiah continues to use Edom to symbolize all who seek to destroy God's people in 63:1.

For it is the day of the LORD's vengeance. The smoke thereof shall go up forever, from generation to generation it shall lie waste. 34:8, 10 Her nobles and princes will not be found there; only wild beasts and owls and vultures shall gather there.

Seek out the book of the LORD and read. 34:16 When we read the book of Isaiah and compare its prophecies with history, we know they were fulfilled. Edom ceased to be a nation after the Romans conquered Palestine in AD 70.

---

[39] Don Shackelford, Ibid., p. 352
[40] Don Shackelford, Ibid., p. 350-351

The wilderness and the solitary place shall be glad; and the desert shall rejoice and blossom as the rose. It shall blossom abundantly and rejoice, even with joy and singing. They shall see the glory of the LORD and the excellency of our God. 35:1-2 When rain comes, desert places are transformed into areas of beautiful wild flowers and other plants. This scene is symbolic of the great changes produced by God's grace in the lives of sinners. Lives that once were empty and selfish become beautiful and a blessing to others. The redeemed shall see the glory and greatness of the LORD and will rejoice with singing.

Strengthen the weak hands and confirm the feeble knees. 35:3 This verse is quoted in Hebrews 12:12 as an exhortation to Christians to strengthen their faith in God during hardships.

Say to them that are of a fearful heart, "Be strong, fear not! Behold, your God will come with vengeance. He will come and save you." Then the eyes of the blind shall be opened, and the ears of the deaf shall be unstopped. 35:4-5 Hailey says, "The eyes that had been closed to God's appeal will be opened to see the salvation offered by Him; the ears that have been deaf to His call will be unstopped to hear and heed His word (cf. 6:9-10)." [41] Shackelford notes, "When John sent his disciples to ask Jesus, 'Are You the Expected One, or shall we look for someone else?' (Matthew 11:3), the Lord replied by citing the words of Isaiah 35:5. This is a clear indication that the glory described is not referring to the physical world, but to the spiritual blessings experienced in Christ." [42]

---

[41] Homer Hailey, Ibid., p. 295
[42] Don Shackelford, Ibid., p. 359

And a highway shall be there ... and it shall be called the way of holiness; the unclean shall not pass over it. 35:8 Isaiah uses the imagery of a highway to describe our access to God. (cf. 11:16; 19:23; 40:3) Our Lord Jesus Christ said, "I am the way, the truth, and the life; no man comes to the Father but by me." (John 14:6)

And the ransomed of the Lord shall return and come to Zion with songs and everlasting joy. 35:10 Those redeemed by the blood of Christ have come to spiritual Mount Zion, the church of the firstborn. (Hebrews 12:22-24) Jesus Christ is "the firstborn from the dead." (Col. 1:18) Their joy is everlasting joy with God in heaven. (Revelation 14:1-5)

Review Questions on Isaiah 28 - 35

1. "Woe to the crown of pride, to the _____ of Ephraim," the northern kingdom of Israel. 28:1

2. The LORD would use the _____ to destroy the kingdom of Israel. 28:2

3. The LORD of hosts would be "a crown of glory" to the _____ of his people. 28:5

4. The prophets and the priests of Judah also had erred through _____ _____. 28:7

5. The word of the LORD is to be learned "_____ upon _____, _____ upon _____."

6. The "precious cornerstone" is _____. 28:16

7. "Ariel" refers to the city of _____, and originally, "Ariel" meant "_____ of God."

8. God said to Ariel, "I will lay _____ against you." 29:3

9. "These people draw near with their _____ and honor me with their _____, but have removed their _____ far from Me." 29:13

10. "Shall the _____ be esteemed as the clay?" 29:16 NKJV

11. "These also that erred in spirit shall come to _____ and they that murmured shall learn _____." 29:24

12. "Woe to the _____ children," says the Lord, "that take _____, but not of me." 30:1

13. "Woe to them that go down to _____ for help." 31:1

14. "Then shall the Assyrian fall with the _____, not of a mighty _____." 31:8

15. "Behold, a king shall reign in _____." 32:1

16. "Your eyes will see the King in his _____." 33:17 "The Lord is our _____, the Lord is our _____ _____, the Lord is our _____." 33:22

17. "Come near, you _____ to hear…for the indignation of the Lord is upon all _____, and his fury against all their _____." 34:1, 2

18. "The eyes of the blind shall be _____, and the ears of the deaf shall be _____." 35:5

19. "A highway shall be there…and it shall be called the way of _____." 35:8

20. "And the ransomed of the Lord shall return and come to Zion with _____ and everlasting _____." 35:10

Hezekiah's Prayers Answered
Isaiah 36 – 39

Isaiah had predicted that Judah would be desolate. The city of Jerusalem, "the daughter of Zion," would be left "as a hut in a garden of cucumbers, as a besieged city." (1:7-8) The LORD answered Hezekiah's prayers by miraculously delivering Jerusalem from the Assyrian army. Hezekiah was twenty-five years old when he became king of Judah, and he reigned for twenty-nine years. His prayers were answered, because "He trusted the LORD God of Israel." (2 Kings 18:1-2, 5) Chapter 38 tells the story of Hezekiah's sickness and recovery, which was also in answer to his prayers. The threat of Babylon is predicted in chapter 39.

Jerusalem Is Besieged
Isaiah 36 – 37

Now it came to pass in the fourteenth year of King Hezekiah, that Sennacherib king of Assyria came up against the defensed cities of Judah and took them. 36:1 When Hezekiah rebelled against the Assyrians by not paying tribute to them (2 Kings 18:7), Sennacherib king of Assyria took all the fortified cities of Judah. Hezekiah sought peace and paid all the tribute that was demanded by the king of Assyria. However, Sennacherib dealt treacherously with Hezekiah. (2 Kings 18:13-16)

And the king of Assyria sent Rab-shakeh from Lachish to Jerusalem to King Hezekiah with a great army. 36:2 Rab-shakeh was not a proper name, but a military title of a high ranking officer in the Assyrian army. This officer was the "field commander." NIV The

Assyrians had just destroyed Lachish, an important city in Judah, 30 miles southwest of Jerusalem. Rab-shakeh came with a great army to Jerusalem and **stood by the conduit of the upper pool in the highway of the fuller's field. 36:2** He was standing in the same place where Isaiah had earlier warned King Ahaz not to put his trust in the Assyrians but in the LORD God of Israel. (7:3, 17)

Three officials of King Hezekiah went out to meet with Rab-shakeh: **Eliakim**, who had replaced Shebna as the steward of the king's house, and **Shebna**, who was demoted to scribe (22:15-23), and **Joah**, the recorder. **36:3**

Rab-shakeh said to them, "Say now to Hezekiah, 'Thus says the great king of Assyria, "What confidence is this wherein you trust?" 36:4 This commander omitted Hezekiah's title as king of Judah, while referring to his ruler as "the great king of Assyria. Sennacherib wanted to know the source of Hezekiah's confidence. **"Now on whom do you trust that you rebel against me?" 36:5** If they were trusting in Egypt to help them, it would be to their pain and suffering. Isaiah had already warned his people not to rely on the Egyptians. (30:1-7) **"But if you say to me, 'We trust in the LORD our God,' is it not he, whose high places and whose altars Hezekiah has taken away?" 36:7** The Assyrians, like others, really worshiped their own power. This field commander believed all gods were alike. He mistakenly believed that Hezekiah had destroyed the LORD's altars, proving that the LORD was powerless. Hezekiah had destroyed idols, but he had restored the worship of the one true God, the only One who had to power to save them.

Rab-shakeh added, **"The LORD said to me, 'Go up against this land and destroy it.'" 36:10** It is doubtful that the LORD had spoken to him. However, he may have heard of Isaiah's prophecy that God was sending the Assyrians as "the rod of his anger" to punish Judah for their sins (10:5-11). Isaiah also had said that God would punish Assyria for its arrogance and greed (10:12-19).

Hezekiah's officials did not want the people on the wall of Jerusalem to be discouraged by the words of Rab-shakeh, so they asked him to speak in the Syrian (Aramaic) language, which was the diplomatic international language. But he refused, saying that his king sent him to speak to the people of Jerusalem, who were doomed for destruction. "He wanted to be understood, for his words were intended to cause panic to those gathered on the city walls for defenses." [43] **36:11-12**

Then Rab-shakeh stood and cried with a loud voice in the Jews' language, and said, "Hear the words of the great king, the king of Assyria. Thus says the king, 'Let not Hezekiah deceive you; for he shall not be able to deliver you. Neither let Hezekiah make you trust in the LORD, saying, "The LORD will surely deliver us; this city shall not be delivered into the hand of the king of Assyria." 'Do not listen to Hezekiah,' for thus says the king of Assyria, 'Make an agreement with me by a present and come out to me and eat every one of his vine and every one of his fig tree and drink every one the waters of his own cistern, until I come and take you away to a land like your own land, a land of corn and wine, a land of bread and vineyards. Beware lest Hezekiah persuade you, saying, "The LORD will deliver us." Has any of the gods of the nations delivered his land out of the hand of the king of Assyria? ... Have they delivered Samaria out of my hand? Who are they among all the gods of these lands that have delivered their land out of my hand, that the LORD should deliver Jerusalem out of my hand?'"

---

[43] Don Shackelford, *Truth for Today Commentary, Isaiah*, p. 373

36:13-20 To be heard by all the people on the wall, Rab-shakeh spoke with a loud voice; to be understood, he spoke in their language. He wanted them to submit to "the great king, the king of Assyria." King Sennacherib stated that they should not put their faith in Hezekiah or even in the LORD to deliver them out of his hand. He deceitfully promised that they would be treated well as exiles, but the truth is their captives were treated harshly. None of the gods of the conquered nations were able to deliver them out of the hands of the Assyrians. Even the gods of Israel had failed to save Samaria. He was demanding that Jerusalem surrender.

King Hezekiah's three officials **answered him not a word, for the king's commandment was, saying, "Answer him not." 36:21** Then Eliakim, Shebna, and Joah came to Hezekiah with their clothes torn in anguish and told him the words of Rab-shakeh. **36:22 When King Hezekiah heard it, he tore his clothes, and covered himself with sackcloth, and went into the house of the LORD. 37:1** With signs of distress and humility, Hezekiah went to the temple to pray.

Hezekiah sent Eliakim, Shebna, and the elders of the priests to the prophet Isaiah. These men also were covered with sackcloth. And they said, **"Thus says Hezekiah, 'This day is a day of trouble, and of rebuke, and of blasphemy; for the children are come to the birth, and there is not strength to bring forth. It may be that the LORD your God will hear the words of Rab-shakeh, whom the king of Assyria, his master, has sent to reproach the living God and will reprove the words which the LORD your God has heard. Therefore lift up your prayer for the remnant that is left." 37:2-4** Hezekiah requested that Isaiah pray for the few people left in Judah after the destruction by Sennacherib.

And Isaiah said to them, "Thus shall you say unto your master, 'Thus says the LORD, "Be not afraid of the words that you have heard, with which the servants of the king of Assyria have blasphemed me. Behold, I will send a spirit upon him, and he shall hear a rumor and return to his own land; and I will cause him to fall by the sword in his own land." 37:6-7 Faith in God replaces fear. The apostle Paul would write, "If God is for us, who can be against us?" (Romans 8:31)

Rab-shakeh returned and found the king of Assyria warring against Libnah; for he had heard that he was departed from Lachish. 37:8 After conquering Lachish, the Assyrians fought against Libnah, a city ten miles to the north.

When the king of Assyria heard that Tirhakah king of Ethiopia had come to make war against him, **he sent messengers to Hezekiah, saying, "Thus you shall speak to Hezekiah king of Judah, saying, 'Let not your God in whom you trust deceive you, saying, "Jerusalem shall not be given into the hand of the king of Assyria." 'Behold! You have heard what the kings of Assyria have done to all lands by destroying them utterly; and shall you be delivered? Have the gods of the nations delivered them which my fathers have destroyed?"' 37:9-12** In chapter 18, Isaiah had spoken of the Ethiopians and of their desire to make an alliance with Judah. Tirhakah king of Ethiopia was coming against the Assyrians with an army from Egypt. At that time, the Ethiopians ruled Egypt's twenty-fifth dynasty. Later, Tirhakah would be the last Pharaoh in this dynasty. Sennacherib tried to force Hezekiah to surrender, so he would not have to fight on two fronts. He sent messengers to the king of Judah, saying, **"Let not your God in whom you trust deceive you."**

And Hezekiah received the letter from the hand of the messengers and read it; and Hezekiah went up to the house of the LORD and spread it before the LORD. 37:14 The king of Judah showed his trust in his God by going to the temple and presenting this blasphemous letter to the LORD for him to answer. His prayer is one of the great prayers recorded in the Bible.

Hezekiah prayed to the LORD saying, **"O LORD of hosts, God of Israel, who dwells between the cherubim, you are the God, even you alone, of all the kingdoms of the earth. You have made heaven and earth. Incline your ear, O LORD, and hear; open your eyes, O LORD, and see. And hear all the words of Sennacherib, which has sent to reproach the living God. Of a truth, LORD, the kings of Assyria have laid waste all the nations and their countries and have cast their gods into the fire; for they were no gods, but the work of men's hands, wood and stone. Therefore, they have destroyed them. Now therefore, O LORD our God, save us from his hand, that all the kingdoms of the earth may know that you are the LORD, even you only." 37:15-20** Hezekiah's prayer exalts the LORD above all heavenly beings and earthly kingdoms. His power has been demonstrated as Creator of heaven and earth. He prays for God to respond to Sennacherib's blasphemy. The gods of other countries were not able to save their people because they were not gods. Hezekiah prays that God would save His people so all the kingdoms of the earth would see His power and know that He, the LORD, is the only God.

Then Isaiah sent a message from the LORD to Hezekiah in answer to his prayer concerning Sennacherib king of Assyria. **"The virgin, the daughter of Zion, has despised you, and laughed you to scorn; the daughter of Jerusalem has shaken her head against you. Whom have you reproached and blasphemed? And against** whom have you exalted your voice and lifted up your eyes on high? Even against the Holy One of Israel." **37:21-23** The word "virgin" is used to describe Zion indicating that Jerusalem had not been captured. Sennacherib had reproached and blasphemed the **Holy One of Israel.** His boasts of conquests are given in **verses 24-25.** But the LORD asks him, **"Have you not heard long ago how I have done it; and of ancient times, that I have formed it? Now I have brought it to pass that you should be to lay waste defensed cities into ruinous heaps." 37:26** God had given Sennacherib the power to punish and destroy cities and nations, because of their wickedness. God's purpose will be done.

And the LORD said to Sennacherib, **"But I know your abode, and your going out and your coming in, and your rage against me. Because your rage against me … is come up into my ears, therefore I will put my hook in your nose and my bridle in your lips, and I will turn you back by the way by which you came." 37:28-29** The LORD was seeing Sennacherib's every move and was hearing his every word. After serving God's purpose, he would be punished for his arrogance. He would return home without taking Jerusalem.

God gave a reassuring sign to Hezekiah, saying, **"You shall eat this year such as grows of itself." 37:30** By God's providence the people of Judah would have food to eat until they returned to planting and harvesting of crops. Then they would be an established, fruitful nation again. **"And the remnant that is escaped of the house of Judah shall again take root downward, and bear fruit upward. For out of Jerusalem shall go forth a remnant, and they that escape out of mount Zion; the zeal of the LORD of hosts shall do this." 37:31-32**

Therefore, thus says the LORD concerning the king of Assyria. "He shall not come into this city, nor shoot an arrow there, nor come before it with shields, nor cast a bank against it. By the way he came, by the same he shall return, and shall not come again into this city," says the LORD, "For I will defend this city to save it for my own sake, and for my servant David's sake." 37:33-35 God assured Hezekiah and those with him that Jerusalem would be delivered; and not even one arrow would be shot. Sennacherib would return to Assyria, never to come again to Jerusalem. God would defend the city and save it, because of the promise he had made to David to establish his seed and the throne of his kingdom forever. (2 Samuel 7:12-16) This promise was to be fulfilled in Jesus Christ. (Luke 1:31-33)

Then the angel of the LORD went forth and smote in the camp of the Assyrians 185,000; and when they arose early in the morning, behold, they were all corpses. So, Sennacherib king of Assyria departed, and went and returned and dwelt at Nineveh. 37:35-36 The destruction of the Assyrian army came immediately after Isaiah's reassuring message was delivered to Hezekiah, because we read in 2 Kings 19:35, "And it came to pass **that night** the angel of the LORD went out and smote in the camp of the Assyrians 185,000." Hailey notes, "Further evidence of the miraculous nature of the slaughter of the Assyrians is that those in the camp who were not slain were ignorant of what happened until morning, for it is said, *And when men arose early in the morning, behold, these were all dead bodies.*" [44] With only a remnant of soldiers, Sennacherib went back to Assyria in defeat.

---

[44] Homer Hailey, *A Commentary on Isaiah*, p. 313

Twenty years later, as Sennacherib was worshiping in the house of Nisroch his god, two of his sons murdered him with the sword, **and they escaped into the land of Armenia. And Esar-haddon his son reigned in his stead.** 37:37 Hezekiah trusted in the LORD, and God delivered Jerusalem from Sennacherib's hand. Sennacherib's god could not save him from his own sons.

Hezekiah's Sickness and Recovery

In those days, Hezekiah became seriously sick, and the prophet Isaiah came to him and said, **"Thus says the LORD, 'Set your house in order; for you shall die and not live.'" Then he turned his face to the wall and prayed to the LORD, saying, "I beseech thee, O LORD, remember now how I have walked before you in truth and with a perfect heart, have done that which is good in your sight." And Hezekiah wept bitterly.** 38:1-3 In those days refers to the time that Sennacherib was threatening Jerusalem (v. 6). Isaiah told Hezekiah to prepare for his death, because he would **die and not live.** We also should prepare for death, because we all will die and not live, "as it is appointed unto men once to die, but after this the judgment." (Hebrews 9:27) Hezekiah had lived a good life. He had removed idols from Judah (2 Kings 18:4-6) and restored the worship of the LORD in the temple (2 Chron. 29). Hezekiah was distressed by the prophet's words, but instead of becoming unfaithful and bitter, he turned to God in prayer. Hailey says, "His plea is based not on self-righteousness, but on his life of faith ... Hezekiah's petition was not altogether selfish, for he was concerned about his nation as well. The world was in turmoil. Judah was at war with Sennacherib." [45] Hezekiah felt his nation needed him at this time.

---

[45] Hailey, Ibid., p. 315

Then the word of the LORD came to Isaiah, saying, "Go, and say to Hezekiah, 'Thus says the LORD, the God of David your father, "I have heard your prayer, I have seen your tears; behold, I will add unto your days fifteen years. And I will deliver you and this city out of the hand of the king of Assyria, and I will defend this city." 38:4-6** Hezekiah's near-death experience came before the siege of Jerusalem: **"I will deliver you and this city."** It was faith-building. If God could save him from death, He could also save Jerusalem from destruction. This explains Hezekiah's trust in God when he received Sennacherib's blasphemous letter. "Consider it all joy, my brethren, when you encounter various trials, knowing that the testing of your faith produces endurance." (James 1:2-3) NASB

"And this shall be a sign to you from the LORD that the LORD will do this thing that he has spoken. Behold, I will bring again the shadow of the degrees, which is gone down in the sundial." ... So the sun returned ten degrees. 38:7-8 Hezekiah was learning there is nothing too hard for the LORD. (Genesis 18:14; Jeremiah 32:27-42) Hezekiah's psalm of thanksgiving to God for sparing his life is in **38:9-22**. He describes his feelings when facing death in verses 9-14. Then he praises God for his recovery, saying, **"What shall I say? He has both spoken to me and ... has done it." 38:15** The king had to experience bitterness in order to find **peace.** Hezekiah says, **"Behold, for peace I had great bitterness, but you have in love to my soul delivered it from the pit of corruption; for you have cast all my sins behind your back." 38:17**

"The LORD was ready to save me. Therefore, we will sing my songs to the stringed instruments all the days of our life in the house of the LORD." 38:20 This is the only place in the book of Isaiah that "stringed instruments" are mentioned. Hezekiah and the nation of Judah would sing songs to the stringed instruments in the temple along with animal sacrifices, as they were commanded under the old covenant. (2 Chronicles 29:20-25; Psalm 150) However, when Isaiah speaks of the new covenant that brings salvation, the command is only to sing. (Isaiah 12:3-5; Isaiah 24:14; Isaiah 26:19; Isaiah 35:10; Isaiah 42:10; and Isaiah 51:11. If stringed instruments were to accompany these songs, Isaiah would have said so, as Hezekiah did in this verse.

Visitors from Babylon

At that time Merodach-baladan son of Baladan, king of Babylon, sent letters and a present to Hezekiah; for he had heard that he had been sick and was recovered. 39:1 Merodach-baladan, king of Babylon, rebelled against the Assyrians in 703 BC. About this time, he sent a delegation to Jerusalem with letters of congratulations to Hezekiah on his recovery from his recent sickness, along with a present. Shackelford says, "However, the real reason, no doubt, was to encourage Hezekiah to revolt against Assyria." [46]

And Hezekiah was pleased with them and showed them the house of his treasures—the silver and gold, the spices and precious ointment, and all his armory— all that was found among his treasures. There was nothing in his house or in all his dominion that Hezekiah did not show them. 39:2 [NKJV] This proves that Hezekiah's sickness and recovery was before he was stripped of all his wealth of silver and gold to pay tribute to Sennacherib for his rebellion against him (2 Kings 18:14-16); and this explains his rebellion against Assyria. Hezekiah felt honored to receive letters and a gift from such an

---

[46] Shackelford, Ibid., p. 39

important king. The flattery of the Babylonians caused him to be tempted with pride to show them all the wealth of his kingdom and its armaments.

Then Isaiah the prophet went to King Hezekiah, and said to him, "What did these men say, and from where did they come to you?" So Hezekiah said, "They came to me from a far country, from Babylon." 39:3 ^(NKJV) He was flattered by their coming such a long distance to see him. Then Isaiah asked, **"What have they seen in your house?" And Hezekiah answered, "All that is in my house they have seen: there is nothing among my treasures that I have not shown them." 39:4** The prophet already knew the answers, but he wanted the king to think about the consequences of what he had done.

Then Isaiah said to Hezekiah, "Hear the word of the LORD of hosts: 'Behold, the days come that all that is in your house ... shall be carried to Babylon; nothing shall be left,' says the LORD." 39:5-6 The Babylonians would carry away all of the wealth of Judah before destroying Jerusalem in 586 BC. **"And they shall take away some of your sons who descend from you, and they shall become eunuchs in the palace of the king of Babylon." 39:7** This prophecy was fulfilled when Daniel, Hananiah (Shadrach), Mishael (Meshach), and Azariah (Abed-Nego) were taken to Babylon to be trained as government officials in their kingdom. (Daniel 1:3-7)

Then Hezekiah said to Isaiah, "Good is the word of the LORD which you have spoken." He said moreover, **"For there shall be peace and truth in my days." 39:8** Hezekiah humbly submitted to the word of God and expressed his gratitude for the peace that he would enjoy.

Review Questions on Isaiah 36 – 39

1. Why did the king of Assyria attack all the cities of Judah? _____
   _____

2. The king of Assyria sent Rab-shakeh to Jerusalem with a great _____. 36:2

3. This Assyrian officer spoke with a loud voice in the language of the _____ so he could be _____ and _____.

4. He told them not to trust in the _____ to deliver them. 36:15

5. What did King Hezekiah do when he heard these blasphemous words of the Assyrians? _____
   _____

6. Who reassured Hezekiah that the Lord would save Jerusalem? 37:6 _____

7. The king of Assyria sent messengers to Hezekiah with a _____ warning him not to trust his _____. 37:10-14

8. Hezekiah prayed for the Lord to save His people so that all the _____ of the earth may know that the Lord is the only _____. 37:15-20

9. How did God answer Hezekiah's prayer? 37:37-38
   _____
   _____

10. When Hezekiah was sick, what was Isaiah's message? 38:1 _____
    _____

11. God answered Hezekiah's prayer by adding to his life _____ years. 38:5

12. What did God also promise Hezekiah at this time? 38:6 _____

13. What sign did God give to Hezekiah? 38:7-8
    _____
    _____

14. Hezekiah's _____ is in 38:9-22.

15. The king of _____ sent a letter and a gift to Hezekiah when he recovered from his sickness.

16. Hezekiah showed all his _____ to this delegation.

17. What question did Isaiah ask Hezekiah concerning these visitors? 39:4 _____
    _____

18. In the future, some of the sons that would descend from Hezekiah would be _____ in the palace of the king of _____. 39:6-7

Part II

Prophecies of Comfort

Isaiah 40 - 66

The Lord Brings Comfort
Isaiah 40 – 43

Isaiah closes the first part of his book predicting that the treasures of the kingdom of Judah would be carried away to Babylon. (39:6) However in chapters 40 – 66, the LORD promises hope for the future.

"Comfort ye, comfort ye my people," says your God. "Speak comfortably to Jerusalem and cry unto her, that her warfare is accomplished, that her iniquity is pardoned; for she has received of the LORD's hand double for all her sins." 40:1-2 God instructs his spokesmen, the prophets, to comfort his people. God would not abandon them in a foreign land. **Speak comfortably** literally means "speak to the heart." Jerusalem stands for God's surviving remnant. Her **warfare**, the hardships and sufferings in exile, would be over. She would be **pardoned** when she returned to God in repentance and obedience, according to Deuteronomy 30:2-3, 8-10. God's blessings are greater than his punishment for sins, **for she has received of the LORD's hand double for all her sins**. Jerusalem would be restored to even greater glory. (Haggai 2:9) Christ, the last spokesman, speaks comfort to God's people. (Heb. 1:1-3) The threefold message in Isaiah 40:2 is also for the redeemed of all nations. It is an outline of the remaining chapters in the book: Her warfare is ended (40 - 48). Her iniquity is pardoned (49 - 57). She has received double blessings from the LORD's hand (58 - 66).

The voice of him that cries in the wilderness, "Prepare the way of the LORD, make straight in the desert a highway for our God." 40:3 All four gospel writers use this verse to refer to the work of John the Baptist. (Matthew 3:3; Mark 1:3; Luke 3:4; and John 1:23)

Although John was born about six months before Jesus (Luke 1:36-44), John said that Jesus was "before him" and that he is "the Son of God." (John 1:30, 34) John introduced Jesus to the people, by saying, "Behold the Lamb of God, who takes away the sin of the world." (John 1:29) Isaiah said that John would prepare the way for "the LORD ... our God." Isaiah added, **"And the glory of the LORD shall be revealed." 40:5** If the Jews had believed Isaiah, they would not have accused Jesus of blasphemy.

The messenger in the wilderness will warn the people. **"Surely the people are grass. The grass withers, the flower fades, but the word of our God shall stand forever." 40:7-8** Our life on earth is like grass; it withers away and comes to an end, but God's word will last forever. Peter quotes these words and says, "And this is the word which by the gospel is preached unto you." (1 Pet. 1:24-25) Jesus said, "Heaven and earth shall pass away, but my words shall not pass away." (Matthew 24:35)

The Greatness of Our God
Isaiah 40:9 – 41:29

O Zion, that brings good tidings, get up into the high mountain; O Jerusalem, that brings good tidings, lift up your voice with strength; lift it up, be not afraid; say to the cities of Judah, "Behold your God!" 40:9 After their exile in Babylon, God's people would return to Jerusalem. John the Baptist would announce, "Behold your God!" The law (the new covenant) would go forth from Zion, and the word of God (the gospel) would go forth from Jerusalem. (2:3) This prophecy is fulfilled in the New Testament. (Luke 24:49; Acts 1:8, 12; and Acts 2:4, 11) The Lord's church is called Zion, the heavenly Jerusalem, in Hebrews 12:22-23. It is to lift up its voice without fear and proclaim the good tidings, "Behold your God!"

Behold, the Lord GOD will come with a strong hand, and his arm shall rule for him; behold, his reward is with him, and his work before him. 40:10 Jesus Christ is declared to be "the ruler over the kings of the earth" in Revelation 1:5. ᴺᴷᴶⱽ Jesus says, "Behold, I come quickly; and my reward is with me to give every man according as his work shall be." (Rev. 22:12)

He shall feed his flock like a shepherd; he shall gather the lambs with his arm. 40:11 Jesus said, "I am come that they might have life and that they might have it more abundantly. I am the good shepherd." (John 10:10-11) After scattering his people because of their sins, God would gather a faithful remnant as they returned to Jerusalem. This prophecy is ultimately fulfilled in Jesus, who said, "And other sheep I have, which are not of this fold; them also I must bring, and they shall hear my voice; and there shall be one fold and one shepherd." (John 10:16) They would come from all nations—Jews and Gentiles.

Who has measured the waters in the hollow of his hand, and meted out heaven with the span? Who has directed the spirit of the LORD, or being his counselor has taught him? With whom took he counsel, and who instructed him, and taught him knowledge, and showed him the way of understanding? 40:12-14 The greatness of God can be seen in his rule over his creation. There is no one like God. Paul uses verse 13 in Romans 11:34 and in 1 Corinthians 2:16.

Behold, the nations are as a drop of a bucket ... All nations before him are as nothing. 40:15, 17 The powers of the nations are nothing when compared with the power of God. The forests of **Lebanon** could not provide enough wood or animals for the **burnt offering**

that the L ORD deserves. **40:16 To whom then will you liken God? Or what likeness will you compare to him? 40:18** These are rhetorical questions that introduce the foolishness of making an idol of gold or silver or wood.

Have you not known? Have you not heard? Has it not been told you from the beginning? Have you not understood from the foundations of the earth? It is he that sits upon the circle of the earth, and the inhabitants thereof are as grasshoppers; that stretches out the heaven as a curtain and spreads them out as a tent to dwell in; that brings the princes to nothing; he makes the judges of the earth as vanity. ... "To whom then will you liken me, or shall I be equal?" says the Holy One. 40:21-25 From the creation of the world, the LORD has ruled from his throne above the affairs of the earth. Men are as grasshoppers or other insects in comparison with God. God gives power to rulers, and he takes it away, according to Daniel 2:20-21. The decisions and the verdicts of human judges are not final; God is the supreme judge. He has no equal.

Lift up your eyes on high and behold who has created these things that bring out their host by number; he calls them all by names. 40:26 God created the stars and calls them all by name. In exile the people would be saying, **"My way is hid from the LORD." 40:27** They would think that either God was too far away or he was indifferent to their ways.

Have you not known? Have you not heard that the everlasting God, the LORD, the Creator of the ends of the earth, faints not, neither is weary? There is no searching of his understanding. He gives power to the faint; and to them that have no might he increases strength. Even the youths shall faint and be weary,

and the young men shall utterly fall. But they that wait upon the LORD shall renew their strength; they shall mount up with wings as eagles; they shall run and not be weary; and they shall walk, and not faint.** 40:28-31 Our God is eternal and the Creator of all things. He is always alert to our conditions. His understanding of us is beyond our comprehension. He gives us power and strength. The apostle Paul said, "I can do all things through Christ who **strengthens** me." (Philippians 4:13) Peter wrote, "The God of all grace, who has called us unto his eternal glory by Christ Jesus, after you have suffered a while, make you perfect, establish, **strengthen**, settle you. To him be glory and dominion forever and ever. Amen." (1 Peter 5:10-11)

The Almighty God says, **"Keep silence before me, O islands; and let the people renew their strength; let them come near; then let them speak; let us come near together to judgment. Who raised up the righteous man from the east, called him to his foot, gave the nations before him, and made him rule over kings? He gave them as the dust to his sword ... Who has wrought and done it, calling the generations from the beginning? I the LORD, the first and with the last, I am he. The isles** (coastlands) **saw it and feared; the ends of the earth were afraid."** 41:1-5 Almighty God rules over the nations of the earth. We will learn in Isaiah 44:28 - 45:7 that Cyrus king of Persia was the "man from the east" who would conquer kings. One hundred and fifty years before Cyrus conquered Babylon, the LORD had called him by name to be his servant. God is in control of the rise and fall of nations. He judges the kingdoms of men.

"But you, Israel, are my servant, Jacob whom I have chosen, the seed of Abraham my friend." 41:8

Israel was God's servant nation through which he would bring the Savior into the world. (Romans 9:4-5) Abraham is called God's friend here and also in 2 Chronicles 20:7 and in James 2:23. **"You are my servant; I have chosen you and not cast you away. Fear not, for I am with you; be not dismayed, for I am your God. I will strengthen you; yes, I will uphold you with the right hand of my righteousness ... They that war against you shall be as nothing ... For I the LORD your God will hold your right hand, saying to you, 'Fear not; I will help you.'" 41:9-13** Christians have the same confidence in the Lord, according to Romans 8:31-32 and Hebrews 13:5-6.

"When the poor and needy seek water, and there is none, and their tongue fails for thirst, I the LORD will hear them, I the God of Israel will not forsake them." 41:17 God provides for his people. **41:18-20**

"Present your case," says the LORD. "Bring forth your strong reasons," says the King of Jacob. "Let them bring forth and show us what will happen; let them show the former things, what they were, that we may consider them, and know the latter end of them." 41:21-22 NKJV God calls upon the idols to show reasons for believing in them. They are powerless to predict the future or explain the consequences of the past. Only the true God of heaven has that power.

"I have raised up one from the north, and he shall come; from the rising of the sun he shall call upon my name." 41:25 God stirred up Cyrus king of Persia by accurately predicting his conquest of the city of Babylon. Cyrus came from the north in his attack. He was from the rising of the sun; for Persia was east of Babylon. Cyrus acknowledged that "the LORD God of heaven" had given him the kingdoms of the earth. (Ezra 1:1-4) **"Who has declared from the beginning, that we may know?" 41:26** Only the LORD has been able to predict the future so that we may know. Their idols were unable to do that.

The LORD's Two Servants
Isaiah 42

"Behold, my servant, whom I uphold, my elect, in whom my soul delights. I have put my Spirit upon him; he shall bring forth judgment to the Gentiles. He shall not cry, nor lift up, nor cause his voice to be heard in the street. A bruised reed he shall not break, and the smoking flax he shall not quench. He shall bring forth judgment unto the truth. He shall not fail nor be discouraged, till he has set judgment in the earth; and the isles shall wait for his law." 42:1-4 These words are quoted and applied to Christ in Matthew 12:18-21. The Messiah is the first servant of the LORD mentioned in this chapter. The Hebrew word Messiah means "anointed," and Christ is the Greek for "anointed." He is God's chosen one, his **elect**. God put his Spirit upon Jesus at the time his baptism. (Matthew 3:16) God's Servant would be gentle in bringing justice to the nations, according to the truth. He would not be discouraged in his mission to save lost mankind.

"I, the LORD, have called you in righteousness, and will hold your hand, and will keep you, and give you for a covenant of the people, for a light of the Gentiles; to open the blind eyes, to bring out the prisoners from the prison, and them that sit in darkness out of the prison house." 42:5-7 As the Creator of the heavens, God is speaking to his servant, the Messiah. God called Christ in righteousness, so that the gift of righteousness could be given through him. (Romans 5:17; 1 Cor. 1:30)

God was with Jesus and protected him during his ministry. The new covenant was made possible by the shedding of Christ's blood, "the blood of the everlasting covenant." (Hebrews 13:20) Christ would be the light that would call all the nations out of darkness. (1 Peter 2:9-10) He would open the eyes of both the physically and the spiritually blind. He would deliver those held captive by sin and death. (Colossians 1:13; Hebrews 2:14-15)

"Behold, the former things are come to pass, and the new things I do declare; before they spring forth I tell you of them." 42:9 God's prophecies in the past have been fulfilled exactly as he had predicted. This should assure us of the prophecies he has made for the future.

Sing unto the LORD a new song and his praise from the end of the earth. 42:10 He shall prevail against his enemies. 42:13 The new song is one of victory in God's Servant, the Messiah; it will be sung in heaven. (Rev. 14:3)

"I have long time held my peace. I have been still and refrained myself. Now I will cry ... I will destroy. 42:14 I will make darkness light before them, and crooked places straight. These things I will do to them, and not forsake them." 42:16 God's second servant is Israel, the entire nation including Judah. (42:14-25) It is the deaf and blind servant. (v. 19) This second servant is identified as "Israel" in verse 24. Although Israel was God's chosen nation to bring the Messiah into the world (41:8), the nation as a whole was deaf when it came to hearing God and was blind when it came to seeing his great works. The LORD had been patient with his chosen nation long enough. He had to punish and purify his people, but he would not forsake them. The Assyrians would scatter the kingdom of Israel among the Gentiles, and the Babylonians would destroy

Jerusalem and carry the remaining Jews away to Babylon. But God would not forsake his righteous remnant. Cyrus would allow those of all of Israel to return to Jerusalem to rebuild the city and God's temple. (Ezra 1:1-4) The Messiah would give them light and guidance. The gospel of Christ provides light and makes straight the way. (2 Timothy 1:10) **Who among you will give ear to this? Who will listen and hear for the time to come? 42:23** A righteous remnant would hear God's reason for their sufferings and believe God's hope for the future.

Who gave Jacob for spoil and Israel to the robbers? Did not the LORD, he against whom we have sinned? For they would not walk in his ways, neither were they obedient to his law. Therefore, he has poured upon him the fury of his anger, and the strength of his battle. 42:24-25 When calamities come, people often ask, "Why? I did not deserve this!" But Isaiah makes it clear that God was punishing his people for their sins.

The Redeemer of Israel
Isaiah 43

But now thus says the LORD that created you, O Jacob, and he that formed you, O Israel, "Fear not for I have redeemed you. I have called you by your name; you are mine." 43:1 God is speaking to his faithful remnant, whom he had redeemed. God gave Jacob his new name **Israel** meaning "**power with God**." (Genesis 32:28) The LORD promised to be with his faithful servant; even when he walked through the fire, he would not be burned. **43:2** This prophesy was literally fulfilled when Shadrach, Meshach, and Abed-nego walked unharmed in the midst of a fire. (Daniel 3:19-27) Those who believe and obey God are the true Israel of God, to whom he says,

"Fear not; for I am with you. I will bring your seed from the east and gather you from the west; I will say to the north, 'Give up,' and to the south, 'Keep not back.' Bring my sons from far, and my daughters from the ends of the earth—even everyone that is called by my name; for I have created him for my glory." 43:5-7 Hailey says, "Though this passage speaks of the return of the remnant from exile, it certainly also looks beyond to the gathering of all people called by God's name. This is accomplished only under the Servant Jesus Christ, whom God appointed to the task." [47] Christians, "a new creation" for God's glory, are called by his name. (2 Cor 5:11; Peter 2:9-10; James 2:7)

Bring forth the blind people that have eyes, and the deaf that have ears. 43:8 Hailey observes, "Though blind and deaf, Israel has eyes and ears with which to see and hear if only they will; the Lord seeks to open their eyes and ears by pointing out the wondrous works He has performed through them." [48]

"You are my witnesses," says the LORD, "and my servant whom I have chosen, that you may know and believe in me, and understand that I am he; before me there was no God formed, neither shall there be after me. I, even I, am the LORD, and beside me there is no savior. I have declared and have saved." 43:10-12 There is only one God, and he alone has the power to save.

Thus says the LORD, your redeemer, the Holy One of Israel: "For your sake I have sent to Babylon and brought down all their nobles." 43:14 Long before he sent Cyrus to bring down the Babylonian Empire, God spoke of his conquest as an accomplished fact. After their

---

[47] Homer Hailey, *A Commentary on Isaiah,* p. 363
[48] Hailey, Ibid., p. 362

deliverance from exile in Babylon, the redeemed would serve as witnesses that the LORD is the only true God. They would worship idols no more.

"Behold, I will do a new thing, now it shall spring forth; shall you not know it? I will even make a way in the wilderness." 43:19 The comforting prophecy began, "The voice of him that cries in the wilderness, 'Prepare the way of the LORD, make straight in the desert a highway for our God.'" (40:3) John the Baptist prepared the way for Christ, the True Servant, who would establish a new covenant with God's people. **"This people I have formed for myself; they shall show forth my praise." 43:21**

"But you have not called upon me, O Jacob; but you have been weary of me, O Israel." 43:22 In contrast with God's chosen people who praise him (v. 21), physical Israel was weary of the LORD. God said, **"You have wearied me with your iniquities." 43:24**

"I, even I, am he that blots out your transgressions for my own sake, and will not remember your sins." 43:25 God is pleading with physical Israel to turn away from their wickedness and sins, and seek his forgiveness. He alone is able to remove sins. He is not willing that anyone should perish but that everyone would come to repentance. (2 Peter 3:9) When he provides the Savior, will they know it? (v. 19) In Christ's new covenant their sins would be remembered no more. (Jeremiah 31:31-34) The LORD requests, **"Put me in remembrance." 43:26**

However, because of their sins, the LORD had **given Jacob to the curse, and Israel to reproaches. 43:28**

Review Questions on Isaiah 40 – 43

1. What is the first word in Isaiah 40:1?
   _____

2. The threefold message to spiritual Jerusalem which also serves as an outline of the second part of Isaiah:
   (1) Her warfare is _____ (Isaiah 40-48)
   (2) Her iniquity is _____ (Isaiah 49-57)
   (3) She has received _____ (Isaiah 58-66)

3. The voice in the wilderness saying, "Prepare the way of the LORD," was the voice of _____ _____. 40:3

4. "The grass _____, the flower _____, but the word of our God shall _____ _____." 40:8

5. The everlasting God neither _____ nor is _____. 40:28

6. They that wait on the LORD renew their _____. 40:31

7. God raised up _____ from the east and made him rule over kings. 41:2

8. In Isaiah 41: 8, God calls _____ "my servant."

9. "Fear not, for I am _____ you; be not _____." 41:10

10. In Isaiah 42, the LORD's two servants are the _____ and _____.

11. When was the prophecy, "I have put my Spirit upon him," fulfilled? 42:1
    _____

12. The Messiah will establish _____ in the earth. 42:4

13. Christ would be given "as a _____" and "for a _____ to the Gentiles." 42:6

14. Physical Israel was The _____ and _____ servant In Isaiah 42:14-25.

15. Isaiah 43 is about The _____ of Israel.

16. "Fear not; for I have _____ you, I have called you by your _____; you are _____." 43:1

17. Jacob's new name, "Israel" means _____ with God.

18. God speaks of "everyone that is called by my _____; for I have created him for my _____." 43:7

19. Physical Israel had not _____ upon the LORD, and they had been _____ of him. 43:22

20. God said to physical Israel, "You have wearied me with your _____." 43:24

21. Because of their sins, God had "given Jacob to the _____ and Israel to _____." 43:28

The Lord, Your Redeemer
Isaiah 44-48

Israel had been scattered by the Assyrians; and Judah would be exiled to Babylon. Isaiah predicts the restoration of God's people to their homeland. There would be an even greater restoration in the Messiah. He is described in 44:24 and in 48:16-17 as "The LORD, your Redeemer."

"Yet hear now, O Jacob, my servant, and Israel, whom I have chosen. Thus says the LORD who made you and formed you in the womb, who will help you. Fear not, O Jacob, my servant, and you, Jesurun, whom I have chosen." 44:1-2 Jesurun (or Jeshurun) means "upright." God is speaking to the upright—the faithful remnant of Israel. Israel had been scattered among the nations and Judah would be exiled in Babylon, but God would care for them and restore them as a nation.

"I will pour my spirit upon your seed, and my blessing upon your offspring." 44:3 The Spirit of the LORD would revive and bless the nation as water for a thirsty man and for a dry land. His Spirit would be poured out on the day of Pentecost, revealing the salvation that is in Christ. (Acts 2:1-38) Then they would be a "holy nation" unto God. (1 Peter 2:9)

"Thus says the LORD, the King of Israel, and his Redeemer, the LORD of hosts, I am the first and the last, and besides me there is no God." 44:6 The LORD, *Yahweh* – the Existent One, is speaking to Israel, which had been scattered and exiled for worshiping idols, false gods. The eternal God of heaven is the King of Israel and the Redeemer of Israel. He would prove to his people that he is the only true God. After the exile in Babylon, they would no longer worship idols. He alone is able to predict the future and have his prophecies totally fulfilled. God concludes, **"You are my witnesses. Is there a God besides me?" 44:8**

They that make a graven image are all of them vanity ... and they are their own witnesses. They see not, nor know, that they may be ashamed. Who has formed a god, or molten a graven image that is profitable for nothing? 44:9-10 The prophet shows the foolishness in making an image to worship. An idol cannot see or know anything. A graven image made by man is worthless. A man cuts down a tree. He burns part of the tree in order to warm himself and cook his food. And with the remaining part, he makes a graven image and worships it as his god. **44:14-17** Anything made is inferior to its maker. Why worship something that is dependent upon man for its existence?

"Remember these things, O Jacob and Israel; for you are my servant; I have formed you." 44:21 Idols were formed by man, but the LORD had formed and made Israel into a nation that would be his servant. He would take care of them. He alone deserved their worship.

"I have blotted out, as a thick cloud, your transgressions ... Return unto me, for I have redeemed you." 44:22 As a thick dark cloud, their sins had separated them from God. (Isaiah 59:2) Just as the wind removes the dark clouds and brings a bright sunny day, the LORD had blotted out their sins. He had redeemed them; they could be his people again. But to enjoy God's blessings of redemption, they had to return to him. Jesus Christ has redeemed us with his blood. (Eph. 1:7; 2:8) But to be God's people and enjoy his blessings (Eph. 1:3), we must return to him in faith and obedience. (Eph. 4:17 – 5:17)

Sing, O ye heavens; for the LORD has done it; shout, you lower parts of the earth: break forth into singing, ye mountains ... for the LORD has redeemed Jacob, and glorified himself in Israel. 44:23 After referring to our "day of redemption" in Ephesians 4:30, we are commanded to be "speaking to yourselves in psalms and hymns and spiritual songs, singing and making melody in your heart to the Lord; giving thanks always for all things unto God and the Father in the name of our Lord Jesus Christ." (Eph. 5:19-20)

Thus says the LORD, your redeemer, and he that formed you from the womb, "I am the LORD that makes all things; that stretches forth the heavens ... that turns wise men backward and makes their knowledge foolish; that confirms the word of his servant and performs the counsel of his messengers, that says to Jerusalem, 'You shalt be inhabited;' and to the cities of Judah, 'You shall be built.'" 44:24-26 The LORD is the Redeemer of Israel. He is the Creator of the heavens and earth. He frustrates the signs of the false prophets and makes fools of the diviners who seek to predict the future. He exposes the foolishness of those that are considered wise. He confirms the prophecies of his messengers by fulfilling them. And now through his prophet Isaiah, God predicts that Jerusalem and the cities of Judah would be rebuilt in order to bring the Messiah into the world to be the Redeemer for all mankind.

"I am the LORD ... that says to the deep, 'Be dry!' And I will dry up your river; that says of Cyrus, 'He is my shepherd, and shall perform all my pleasure; even saying to Jerusalem, "You shall be built;" and to the temple, "Your foundation shall be laid."' 44:24, 27-28 The LORD now reveals that Cyrus would be the conqueror "from the east" (41:2), who would perform

God's desire for the restoration of Jerusalem and the temple. Cyrus was king of Persia (Elam), which was east of Babylon. Isaiah already has described the night in which Cyrus would overthrow the kingdom of Babylon in 21:1-9. (cf. Daniel 5) The prophet now tells us that Cyrus would conquer Babylon by drying up the Euphrates River. Albert Barnes reports, "Cyrus took Babylon by diverting the waters of the river Euphrates, and thus leaving the bed of the river dry, so that he could march his army under the walls of the city." [49] Hailey says, "Cyrus will act as Jehovah's shepherd, seeing that Jerusalem and the temple are rebuilt and His flock restored to their proper homeland. Deliverer and deliverance are determined in the secret counsel of the Almighty, which is fulfilled in His own time." [50] This prophecy was made "a century and a half before the event." [51] Cyrus gave the decree for rebuilding Jerusalem and the temple. (Ezra 1:1-4; Daniel 9:25)

"Thus says the LORD to his anointed, to Cyrus, whose right hand I have held, to subdue nations before him ... 'I will go before you and make the crooked places straight; I will break in pieces the gates of brass and cut in sunder the bars of iron. And I will give you the treasures of darkness and hidden riches of secret places that you may know that I, the LORD, who call you by your name, am the God of Israel. For Jacob my servant's sake, and Israel my elect, I have even called you by your name; I have surnamed you, though you have not known me. I am the LORD, and there is none else, there is no God beside me.'" 45:1-5
God had anointed (or appointed) Cyrus to carry out the restoration of Judah. Some modern theologians think that it was humanly impossible for Isaiah to give such a

---

[49] Albert Barnes, *Barnes Notes,* Isaiah 44, Biblesoft
[50] Homer Hailey, *A Commentary on Isaiah,* p. 377
[51] Don Shackelford, *Truth for Today Commentary, Isaiah,* p. 463

detailed prophecy, 150 years in advance; this must have been written after Cyrus took Babylon. But that's the point! God "confirms the word of his servant," by doing the seemingly impossible. (44:26) Only God can tell in details what will occur in the future, and the prophecy is fulfilled in every detail. The idols that men create cannot do that; neither can the false prophets. God had called Cyrus by his name so that he would know that he is the LORD and that there is no other God. In this way, "the LORD stirred up the spirit of Cyrus king of Persia, that he made a proclamation" that allowed the Israelites to rebuild Jerusalem. (Ezra 1:1-4) Such detailed prophecy proves God's power. No wonder Cyrus was stirred to rebuild Jerusalem! The LORD says, **"I form the light and create darkness. I make peace and create calamity; I, the LORD, do all these things." 45:7** NKJV

"Drop down, you heavens from above, and let the skies pour down righteousness; let the earth open, and let them bring forth salvation, and let righteousness spring up together. I, the LORD, have created it." 45:8 God's righteousness was seen in the restoration of Israel, and God's people were brought home. Righteousness and salvation go together. The LORD is the source. The two were completely fulfilled in the coming of the Messiah.

"Woe to him who strives with his Maker! ... Shall the clay say to him who forms it, 'What are you making?' Or shall your handiwork say, 'He has no hands?'" 45:9 NKJV Secular humanists who deny God should take warning. They are striving with their Maker.

Thus says the LORD, the Holy One of Israel, and his Maker, "Ask me of things to come concerning my sons, and concerning the work of my hands ... I have made the earth and created man upon it; I, even my

hands, have stretched out the heavens, and all their host I have commanded." 45:11-12 The LORD declares his universal power in the universe. Hailey says, "Jehovah urges, yea, commands, the critics to ask Him concerning the things to come; what are the Lord's long-range plans for His people? As a Father, Jehovah stands ready to reveal His plans to them and in fact does so in later prophecies." [52]

"I have raised him up in righteousness, and I will direct all his ways; he shall build my city, and he shall let go my captives, not for price or reward," says the LORD of hosts." 45:13 God caused Cyrus to come to power because he would be the one to rebuild God's city of Jerusalem, by allowing the exiles to return home. This was an act of God's righteousness and grace. Notice God said, **"he shall build my city."** Cyrus gave the decree to rebuild Jerusalem—not just the temple. (Daniel 9:25)

The restoration of Israel will cause the nations to see God's redemptive work and give up their idols. The Egyptians, the Ethiopians (Cush), and the Sabeans represent those of all the nations who will learn of the true God and will come to serve him. Restored Israel brought into the world the promised Seed by whom all the nations of the earth will be blessed. (Genesis 22:18; Gal. 3:16) These prophecies are fulfilled spiritually in Christ, whom Cyrus foreshadowed. **"Israel shall be saved in the LORD with an everlasting salvation." 45:17** The church is spiritual Israel today. (Galatians 6:14-16)

For thus says the LORD that created the heavens; God himself that formed the earth and made it; he has established it, he created it not in vain, he formed it to be inhabited: "I am the LORD, and there is none else." 45:18 The LORD proves his greatness by his creation and revelation. God created the earth for mankind to live in it.

---

[52] Hailey, Ibid., p. 381

"Assemble yourselves and come together; draw near together, you that are escaped of the nations. Who has declared this from ancient time? Who has told it from that time? Have not I, the LORD? And there is no God else beside me; a just God and a Savior, there is none other. Look unto me, and be saved, all the ends of the earth, for I am God." 45:20-21 The LORD is speaking to the Gentiles that have renounced their idols and have come to Israel to find the true God. They have escaped the curse of foolishly praying to an image of wood that cannot save. The LORD will assemble his people from all over the world.

"I have sworn by myself. The word is gone out of my mouth in righteousness and shall not return. That unto me every knee shall bow, every tongue shall swear. Surely, shall one say, 'In the LORD I have righteousness and strength.' Even to him, shall men come; and all that are angry against him shall be ashamed. In the LORD, shall all the seed of Israel be justified, and shall glory." 45:23-25 The apostle Paul quotes Isaiah 45:23 to prove that everyone shall stand before the judgment seat of God; and every knee shall bow and every tongue confess and swear allegiance to the LORD. (Rom. 14:10-11) On the Judgment Day, only those in Christ will have righteousness and strength. Those who have come to the LORD during their lifetime on earth will be blessed. Even God's enemies will submit to him at the judgment; but to their shame, it will be too late. The "seed of Israel" refers to spiritual Israel. (Galatians 3:26-29)

Bel bows down, Nebo stoops; their idols were upon the beasts ... they are a burden to the weary beasts. 46:1 Idols that were a burden are contrasted with the living God, who bears the burdens of his people. These images

had to bow as they were placed in a lying down position

upon carriages that carried them from place to place. **Bel-Marduk** was the chief god of the Babylonians, and he was also the patron deity of the city of Babylon. **Bel** means lord, master. **Nebo** was their god of wisdom and knowledge and the patron deity of their rulers. "Nebo" is in the names "Nebuchadnezzar" and "Nabonidus," kings of Babylon. These idols could not deliver those that worshiped them, **but they themselves are gone into captivity. 46:2**

"Listen to me, O house of Jacob, and all the remnant of the house of Israel, which are borne by me ... I will bear, even I will carry and will deliver you." 46:3, 4 God is speaking to his faithful remnant. He had borne them from their beginning as his nation, and he would continue to bear them to their redemption in Christ. (Deut. 1:31; Isaiah 53:4)

"To whom will you liken me, and make me equal, and compare me, that we may be alike?" 46:5 The LORD has no equal. Men hire a goldsmith to make an image of gold, and they worship it as their god. But they have to carry their god to his place and stand him up so he will not fall. The image cannot go anywhere. **One shall cry unto him, yet he cannot answer, nor save him out of his trouble. 46:6-7**

To these idolaters, the LORD says, **"Remember this and show yourselves men; bring it again to mind, O ye transgressors. Remember the former things of old. For I am God, and there is none else; I am God, and there is none like me, declaring the end from the beginning." 46:8-10**

**"My counsel shall stand, and I will do all my pleasure: calling a ravenous bird from the east, the man that executes my counsel from a far country; yes, I have spoken it, I will also bring it to pass; I have

purposed it, I will also do it." 46:10b-11 God's pleasure was to bring Cyrus, as a bird of prey from the east of Babylon. He would conquer Babylon and restore Israel to their homeland. God makes his plans for the future and then carries them out exactly according to his purpose many years later.

"Hear me, you stouthearted that are far from righteousness. I bring near my righteousness, it shall not be far off, and my salvation shall not tarry, and I will place salvation in Zion for Israel my glory." 46:12-13 The LORD is speaking to those that are stubborn and unrighteous. His righteousness and salvation were seen in the restoration of the nation of Israel after the Assyrian and Babylonian captivities. God now shows his righteousness and salvation in the gospel of Christ (Romans 1:16-17) and in the church of Christ, spiritual Zion (Hebrews 12:22-24). Righteousness, salvation, and glory are blessings enjoyed by spiritual Israel, the redeemed of all nations. (Galatians 3:26-29; 6:15-16)

"Come down and sit in the dust, O virgin daughter of Babylon. Sit on the ground; there is no throne, O daughter of the Chaldeans ... for you shall no more be called The Lady of Kingdoms." 47:1, 5 The kingdom of Babylon, that was ruled by the Chaldeans, is called a virgin because it had not been molested by other nations. However, the LORD would remove the kingdom of Babylon, just as he had removed the kingdom of Assyria. They had profaned the holy vessels that had been taken from the temple in Jerusalem by drinking wine in them as they praised their gods of gold and silver. (Daniel 5:3-4) The kingdom of Babylon fell to the ground when Belshazzar the king saw the hand writing on the wall of his palace and he was slain by the Medes and Persians. (Daniel 5:5-30)

"I was angry with my people; I have polluted my inheritance and given them into your hand. You showed them no mercy." 47:6 God used Babylon to punish his people for their sins, even allowing Jerusalem and his temple to be destroyed. The Chaldeans were cruel in their treatment of the Jews, including the elderly.

"And you said, 'I shall be a lady forever.' So that you did not lay these things to your heart, neither did remember the latter end of it." 47:7 Keep in mind that God is predicting these events even before Babylon became a powerful kingdom. God is prophesying Babylon's fall, but Babylon did not take it to heart. Instead, she proudly said, "I shall be a lady forever."

"Therefore, hear now this, you that are given to pleasures ... that say in your heart, 'I am, and none else beside me; I shall not sit as a widow, neither shall I know the loss of children.' But these two things shall come to you in a moment in one day: the loss of children and widowhood." 47:8-9 Arrogance preceded Babylon's fall. Babylon now serves as a symbol for the proud, worldly society of man that is given to pleasures and self-adoration. Revelation 18:7-8 applies these verses in Isaiah to our own worldly society of Babylon today.

"For you have trusted in your wickedness. You have said, 'No one sees me.' Your wisdom and your knowledge have perverted you. And you have said in your heart, 'I am, and none else besides me.' Therefore shall evil come upon you." 47:10-11 This description of ancient Babylon also describes the secular humanists today. They trust in their wickedness; they are advocates for sexual immorality and abortion. They glory in their wisdom and knowledge (science). And they deny the existence of God, saying, "No deity will save us; we must save ourselves." Because of their sins and arrogance, calamity and destruction will come upon them suddenly; there will be no escape from God's judgment and wrath. The Chaldeans had trusted in enchantments and astrologers. But the LORD says, **"None shall save you." 47:12-15**

"Hear you this, O house of Jacob, which are called by the name Israel, and are come forth out of the waters of Judah, which swear by the name of the LORD and make mention of the God of Israel, but not in truth, nor in righteousness." 48:1 In this chapter the LORD calls upon his people to listen to him. The family of Jacob was called by the name Israel, which means "power with God." Their waters of life were coming from the tribe of Judah. Although they had been greatly blessed, they had not been faithful to the LORD. They had profaned God's name with their sins. They identified themselves with **the holy city** of Jerusalem and with **the LORD of hosts. 48:2** However, this was not done in truth, because they had turned to idols. They were guilty of the sin of hypocrisy.

"I have declared the former things from the beginning ... and they came to pass." 48:3 God's fulfilled prophecies in the past should cause us to trust him and believe that his prophecies for the future also will be fulfilled. He says, **"I have even from the beginning declared it to you; before it came to pass I showed it to you, lest you should say, 'My idol has done them.'" 48:5** The true and living God of heaven is in control of things—not man or his idols.

"You have heard, see all this; and will you not declare it?" 48:6 They had heard God's prophecies and had seen them come to pass, but instead of confessing the LORD to the nations, they turned to the powerless gods of the pagans and worshiped them.

"**For my name's sake I will defer my anger ... that I do not cut you off. Behold, I have refined you ... I have chosen you in the furnace of affliction. For my own sake, even for my own sake, I will do it; for how should my name be polluted? And I will not give my glory unto another.**" 48:9-11 God would delay his anger against Israel so that his purpose might be completed. He would refine his people in exile, but impurities would remain in the nation. If God had abandoned his people in exile, his name would have been profaned. The people would say that the LORD is powerless to save. And they would give their praises to idols. For his sake he would delay his anger until after the Christ should come and offer eternal salvation to all nations.

"**Hear me. O Jacob and Israel, my called; I am he, I am the first, I also am the last. My hand also has laid the foundation of the earth, and my right hand has spanned the heavens.**" 48:12-13 Israel needed to pay close attention to LORD. He is the one eternal God, the first and the last. He is before all man-made gods, and he will still exist after all idols are gone. The LORD is the great Creator of the heavens and the earth. God called Israel to be his chosen nation in order to carry out his eternal purpose. Therefore, he would deliver his people from captivity in order to bring the Savior into the world. Referring to idols, the LORD asks, "**Which among them has declared these things?**" 48:14 None of their idols had predicted their deliverance.

"**The LORD has loved him; he will do his pleasure on Babylon, and his arm shall be on the Chaldeans. I, even I, have spoken; yes, I have called him, I have brought him, and shall make his way prosperous.**" 48:14-15 God is speaking of Cyrus, whom he called by name. (44:28 – 45:4) He loved Cyrus by choosing him to restore the Jews to their homeland. When this was fulfilled 150 years later, the Jews knew that the LORD is the only true God.

"Come near to me, hear this: I have not spoken in secret from the beginning, from the time that it was, there I am. And now the Lord GOD and his Spirit have sent me." 48:16 Just six verses later, in 49:1, the speaker who is saying, "Listen to me" is the ideal Servant, the Messiah. The eternal Word was in the beginning with God and was God. (John 1:1) As the Word, he is the messenger and spokesman of the Godhead. When the LORD speaks, he is speaking. The Word was made flesh (John 1:14) in order to become our Redeemer, Christ Jesus. (Rom. 3:24) Translations and Bible scholars are divided over who is speaking in this verse. Some say the speaker is the prophet Isaiah. However the Word who became flesh fits the context. Don Shackelford says, "this verse serves as a bridge to prophecies of the ideal Servant, the Messiah, who becomes prominent in the rest of the book." [53]

Thus says the LORD, your Redeemer, The Holy One of Israel: "I am the LORD your God which teaches you to profit, which leads you by the way you should go. O that you had listened to my commandments! Then your peace would have been as a river and your righteousness as the waves of the sea." 48:17-18 God's teachings are for our benefit and good; they show us the way to live. If only Israel and Judah had heeded God's commandments, they would not have been destroyed; their people would not have been uprooted from their homes and carried away into exile. If only they had listened to God, they would have had both peace and righteousness.

---

[53] Don Shackelford, Ibid., p. 494

Go forth from Babylon, flee from the Chaldeans, with a voice of singing declare, tell this, utter it even to the end of the earth; say, "The LORD has redeemed his servant Jacob." And they thirsted not when he led them through the deserts, he caused the waters to flow out of the rock also, and the waters gushed out. 48:20-21 The return to their homeland would be a time of great joy. Just as God had provided for their fathers during the Exodus from Egypt, he would take care of the captives returning from Babylon.

The chapter concludes with this warning: **"There is no peace," says the LORD, "unto the wicked." 48:22** Israel and Judah learned this important lesson the hard way.

Review Questions on Isaiah 44 – 48

1. God is "the LORD, your _____," according to Isaiah 44:24 and in 48:17.

2. The LORD of hosts was the _____ of Israel and also his _____. 44:6

3. Isaiah tells of a man who cuts down a tree and uses part of it to _____ himself and _____ his food and the other part to make _____.

4. "I have blotted out your _____; return to me, for I have _____ you." 44:22

5. The LORD said of _____, "He is my shepherd, and shall perform all my pleasure: even saying to _____ 'You shall be built' and to the _____ 'your foundation shall be laid.'" 44:28

6. How did Babylon's fall fulfill Isaiah 44:27?
   _____
   _____

7. God said to _____, "I have called you by your name … though you have not known me." 45:1, 4

8. "Woe to him that strives with his _____." 45:9

9. God said of Cyrus, "he shall build my _____, and he shall let go my _____." 45:13

10. Israel shall be saved in the LORD with "an _____ salvation." 45:17

11. "Look to Me and be _____, all the ends of the earth, for I am God, and there is none else." 45:22

12. "Unto Me every _____ shall bow." 45:23

13. In contrast with idols that were carried as a burden, the Lord says, "I will _____, even I will _____, and I will _____ you." 46:4

14. Babylon said, "I will be a lady _____." 47:7

15. The Lord says, "I have declared the _____ things from the beginning ... and they _____ to pass." 48:3

16. Why did God restore Israel to their homeland? 48:11 _____
   _____

17. "I am the Lord your God which teaches you to _____, which leads you by the _____ you should go." 48:17

18. "O that you had listened to My _____! Then your _____ would have been as a river." 48:18

19. God's people were to go from _____ with a voice of _____. 48:20

20. "There is no _____," says the Lord, "for the wicked." 48:22

The Suffering Servant
Isaiah 49 – 53

This section is about the Suffering Servant who will die for our sins. (53:1-6) He is God's "elect" Servant. (42:1-4) He is the Messiah, God's "Anointed One."

"Listen, O isles, to me; and hearken, you people from far. The LORD has called me from the womb; ... he has made mention of my name." 49:1 The Messiah calls upon the people that are afar off, the nations, to pay close attention to his words. As the LORD had called Cyrus by name long before he restored God's people to their homeland, the LORD also has called the Messiah by name, "Immanuel" (God with us), hundreds of years before he came into this world to deliver lost mankind from their bondage of sin. (Isaiah 7:14) And before his birth he was given the name "Jesus" meaning Savior. (Matthew 1:18-21)

"And he has made my mouth like a sharp sword ... And said unto me 'You are my Servant, O Israel, in whom I will show my glory.'" 49:2, 3 Christ has a sharp two-edged sword coming out of his mouth in the symbolic vision of Revelation 1:13-17. In Hebrews 4:12, the word of God is said to be alive and powerful, "sharper than any two-edged sword." Christ conquers with the word of truth. Followers of Christ will use his message of righteousness and peace to advance his kingdom. The apostle Paul wrote in 2 Corinthians 10:4-5, "The weapons we fight with are not the weapons of the world. On the contrary, they have divine power to demolish strongholds. We demolish arguments and every pretention that sets itself up against the knowledge of God, and we take captive every thought to make it obedient to Christ." NIV

God is glorified in Christ (John 17:1-5) and in his church (Ephesians 1:22-23; 3:21). **Israel** means power with God. Christ has that power.

"Then I said, 'I have labored in vain.' ... Yet surely my just reward is with the LORD, and my work with my God." 49:4 NKJV Jesus knew from the beginning of his earthly ministry that he would be rejected, but he continued to faithfully fulfill the mission assigned to him by the LORD. He would "give his life a ransom for many." (Matt. 20:28)

"And he said, 'It is a light thing that you should be my Servant to raise up the tribes of Jacob and to restore the preserved of Israel; I will also give you for a light to the Gentiles, that you may be my salvation unto the end of the earth.'" 49:6 This clearly shows that Christ Jesus is the Servant. Paul quotes Isaiah 49:6 in Acts 13:47 to show that the gospel is to be preached to the Gentiles. The Messiah would bring salvation to all the nations of the world. Restoring the remnant of Israel to God's favor would be a small thing by comparison. He would be the Savior for all men everywhere.

Thus says the LORD, the Redeemer of Israel, and his Holy One, to him whom man despises, to whom the nations abhor ... "Kings shall see and arise, princes also shall worship, because of the LORD who is faithful, the Holy One of Israel, and he shall choose you." 49:7 The Suffering Servant will be "despised and rejected of men." (53:3) However, the LORD has chosen him to be the Messiah, who will be victorious over enemies.

Thus says the LORD, "In an acceptable time have I heard you, and in a day of salvation I have helped you." 49:8a In 2 Corinthians 6:2, Paul quotes this verse and then adds, "Behold, now is the accepted time; behold now is the day of salvation." The Christian Age is the acceptable time and day. "When the fulness of time was come, God sent forth his Son ... to redeem them that were under the law, that we might receive the adoption of sons." (Gal. 4:4-5)

"I will preserve you and give you for a covenant of the people ... to cause to inherit the desolate heritages; that you may say to the prisoners, 'Go forth.'" 49:8b-9 God would protect his Servant during his earthly ministry and raise him from the dead. The death of the Suffering Servant was necessary in order for God to make a new covenant that would take away our sins. (Jer. 31:31-34; Heb. 8:7-12) When Jesus instituted the Lord's Supper, he took the cup and said, "For this is my blood of the new testament, which is shed for many for the remission of sins." (Matt. 26:28) The new covenant provides deliverance from all enemies (54:17) and the blessings of heaven.

"They shall not hunger nor thirst; neither shall the heat nor sun smite them: for he that has mercy shall lead them, even by the springs of water shall he guide them." 49:10 In Revelation 7:16-17, reference is made to this verse in describing heaven. **"Sing, O heavens, and be joyful, O earth. And break forth in singing, O mountains: for the LORD has comforted his people and will have mercy upon his afflicted." 49:13**

But Zion said, "The LORD has forsaken me, and my Lord has forgotten me." 49:14 When the Jews would witness the destruction of Jerusalem and the temple, they would feel forsaken by the LORD. But the LORD answers, **"Can a woman forget her sucking child, that she should not have compassion on the son of her womb?**

Yes, they may forget, yet I will not forget you." 49:15 It is not natural for a mother to forget her young child, even though some do at times. But God will never forget his children.

"Behold, I have engraved you upon the palms of my hands; your walls are continually before me. Your children shall make haste; your destroyers and they that made you waste shall go forth from you." 49:16-17 Hailey says, "When the Lord gave Israel His law, He instructed the people to bind the law as frontlets upon their foreheads, so they would always have His commands in mind, and as signs upon their hands, so they would always see his commands in action (Deut. 6:8). In this way the law was ever before them. Metaphorically, in like manner Jehovah has graven Zion and her walls upon the palms of His hands; thus, *thy walls are continually before me.* From the beginning (Gen. 3), Jehovah had a plan of which He never lost sight—the building of spiritual Zion according to His eternal purpose (Eph. 3:11). In Christ, we have come to that spiritual Zion (Hebrews 12:22-24; Rev. 14:1-5)." [54] In Christ all enemies are conquered.

"Lift up your eyes round about and behold: all these gather together and come to you." 49:18 Zion, the faithful remnant, will see those of all nations coming to her for salvation in Christ. The church is the spiritual bride of Christ (Ephesians 5:23-32), and **as a bride** those coming to her will be worn as **an ornament,** for they are her children. (1 John 5:20-21, Rev. 22:17) The land of old Zion would be a place too small for all of her children; they would need a larger land in which to dwell. **49:19-20** They would need the heavenly new Zion. (Rev. 14:1-3)

---

[54] Homer Hailey, *A Commentary on Isaiah,* 411-412

"**Then you shall say in your heart, 'Who has begotten me these, seeing I have lost my children, and am desolate?'" 49:21** After being scattered, only a remnant of Israel returned to Jerusalem. But now Christians from all nations are "Abraham's seed" by adoption. (Galatians 3:26-29; 4:4-5)

Thus says the Lord GOD, "Behold, I will lift up my hand to the Gentiles, and set my standard to the people; and they shall bring your sons in their arms, and your daughters shall be carried upon their shoulders." 49:22 This describes the gathering of Zion's sons and daughters with the coming of the Christ, the Suffering Servant. The gospel of Christ would be the standard around which the people would be gathered.

"And you shall know that I am the LORD; for they shall not be ashamed that wait for me." 49:23 Seeing Jesus resurrected from the dead, Thomas worshiped him, saying, "My Lord and my God!" (John 20:24-28) Those that wait for God to fulfill his promises will not be disappointed. Zion shall be served by kings and queens.

"Shall the prey be taken from the mighty, or the lawful captive delivered?" 49:24 Is it possible for Zion's remnant to be delivered from their captivity in foreign lands? God answers, **"The captives shall be taken away ... for I will contend with him that contends with you, and I will save your children... And all flesh shall know that I, the LORD, am your Savior and your Redeemer, the mighty One of Jacob." 49:25-26** Shackelford says, "The redemptive, saving power of God was seen in the Exodus and in the return from Exile, and it will be seen in the second coming of the Lord Jesus Christ." [55]

---

[55] Don Shackelford, *Truth for Today Commentary, Isaiah*, p. 505

Thus says the LORD, "Where is the bill of your mother's divorcement? ... Behold, for your iniquities you have sold yourselves, and for your transgressions your mother is put away." 50:1 God had not divorced the kingdom of Judah as his wife. Hailey observes, "The case of the northern kingdom was different. Israel was destroyed (Amos 9:8), caused to cease (Hosea 1:4), given a bill of divorcement (Jer. 3:8) ... By contrast, a bill of divorcement was never given to Judah." [56] There is a difference between "divorcement" and "put away." The Hebrew root word for **divorcement** means "to cut off." Therefore, the ten northern tribes were never restored as a kingdom, but the nation of Judah was restored after the Babylonian captivity. The Jews went into exile because of their sins, but God had not forsaken Zion.

"Is my hand shortened at all, that it cannot redeem? Or have I no power to deliver?" 50:2 The LORD had demonstrated his power to deliver at the time of their exodus from Egypt and also at many other times during their history.

"The Lord GOD has given me the tongue of the learned, that I should know how to speak a word in season to him that is weary. The Lord GOD has opened my ear, and I was not rebellious." 50:4, 5 The LORD's Servant is speaking. (v. 10) The LORD said to Moses, "I will raise them up a Prophet from among their brethren, like unto you, and will put my words in his mouth; and he shall speak to them all that I shall command him. And it shall come to pass, that whosoever will not listen to my words which he shall speak in my name, I will require it of him." (Deut. 18:17-19) The apostle Peter said this prophecy is fulfilled in Jesus. (Acts 3:22-26) Jesus said, "For I have not spoken of myself; but the Father which sent me gave me a command, what I should say and what

---

[56] Homer Hailey, Ibid., p. 415

I should speak." (John 12:49) Christ also said, "He that sent me is with me; the Father has not left me alone, for I always do those things that please him." (John 8:29)

The Servant says, **"I offered my back to those who beat me, my cheeks to those who pulled out my beard; I did not hide my face from mocking and spitting." 50:6** ᴺᴵⱽ Jesus courageously endured these humiliations during his trials before the Jews and the Romans. (Matthew 26:67; 27:27-31)

"For the Lord GOD will help me; therefore ... I shall not be ashamed. He is near that justifies me; who will contend with me?" 50:7, 8a "Christ also suffered for us, leaving us an example, that you should follow in his steps, who did no sin, neither was deceit found in his mouth; who, when he was reviled, reviled not again; when he suffered, he threatened not; but committed himself to him that judges righteously." (1 Peter 2:21-23) Christ knew that he would be victorious over all enemies, because God was with him.

Who is among you that fear the LORD, that obey the voice of his servant, that walk in darkness and have no light? Let him trust in the name of the LORD. 50:10 There will be times as disciples of Christ that we may be unable to see the reason or the end of our sufferings and trials, but we are to continue to trust him who is the light of the world. Jesus said, "I am the light of the world. He that follows me shall not walk in darkness, but shall have the light of life." (John 8:12)

"Behold, all you that kindle a fire, that ... walk in the light of your fire. ... This shall you have of my hand; you shall lie down in sorrow." 50:11 Unbelievers walk in their own light. Shackelford says, "Those who try to live by their own strength, without the help of the Lord, are doomed. Their end is only torment!" [57]

"Listen to me, you that follow after righteousness, you that seek the Lord. Look unto the rock whence you were hewn ... Look to Abraham your father, and to Sarah that bore you; for I called him alone, and blessed him, and increased him." 51:1-2 The Lord is speaking to the faithful remnant of Israel that would be exiled in a foreign land. God brings salvation to those who seek him. Abraham was the rock from which Israel was hewn. God had fulfilled his promise to bless him and make of him a great nation. (Genesis 12:1-3). God also would fulfill the promise he had made to Abraham that in his seed all the nations of the earth would be blessed. (Genesis 22:18)

"For the Lord will comfort Zion ... joy and gladness shall be found therein, thanksgiving and the voice of melody." 51:3 Hailey notes that "this prophecy was fulfilled to only a very limited extent when the Jews returned from exile; full realization of the promise was experienced only with the appearance of the Servant." [58] He offers eternal life in heaven, the restored Eden. (Gen. 2:8-10; Rev. 22:1-5, 17)

"Listen to me, my people; and give ear to me, O my nation: For the law shall proceed from me, and I will make my judgment to rest for a light to the people. My righteousness is near; my salvation is gone forth, and my arms shall judge the people." 51:4-5 Isaiah spoke of this law earlier, saying, "For out of Zion shall go forth the law, and the word of the Lord from Jerusalem." (Isaiah 2:3) The law is the gospel of Christ. As "the perfect law of liberty" (James 1:25), it offers salvation

---

[57] Shackelford, Ibid., p. 511
[58] Hailey, Ibid., p. 422

from sin. In the gospel, the righteousness of God is revealed. (Romans 1:16-17) It would be **a light to the people** and the standard of **judgment**. (John 12:48)

"Lift up your eyes to the heavens, and look upon the earth beneath; for the heavens shall vanish away like smoke, ... but my salvation shall be forever, and my righteousness shall not be abolished." 51:6 Our present heavens and earth will be "dissolved," but righteousness will dwell in "new heavens and a new earth." (2 Peter 3:10-13)

"Listen to me, you that know righteousness, the people in whose heart is my law, fear not the reproach of men." 51:7 God tells his people to pay close attention to his words for the third time. Men will mistreat and insult them, but they are not to fear or fight back. They are to follow the Messiah's example. (50:7-8)

Awake, awake, put on strength, O arm of the LORD! Awake as in the ancient days ... Are You not the arm that has cut Rahab apart and wounded the serpent? Are You not the One who dried the sea ... that made the depths of the sea a road for the redeemed to cross over? 51:9-10 NKJV Shackelford gives this explanation, "**Rahab** (v.9) is a name used by Isaiah to denote Egypt (30:7) It is likely that **the dragon** (serpent) here is a term for Pharaoh (Ezek. 29:3), since the passage has an Exodus theme. The miraculous crossing of the Red Sea during the Exodus (v. 10) demonstrated God's ability to protect His people in dire circumstances (Ex. 14)." [59]

"Therefore the redeemed of the LORD shall return and come with singing unto Zion; and everlasting joy shall be upon their head." 51:11 The return of the remnant from the Babylonian exile would foreshadow the deliverance by the Messiah and the eternal joy to come.

---

[59] Shackelford, Ibid., p. 519

"I, even I, am he that comforts you. Who are you that you should be afraid of a man that shall die ... and forget the LORD your Maker, that has stretched forth the heavens and laid the foundations of the earth?" 51:12-13 The LORD is with his people during their various trials. As the Creator of all things, our Maker is stronger than man. "We may boldly say: 'The LORD is my helper; I will not fear. What can man do to me?'" (Hebrews 13:6, NKJV) "We are more than conquerors through him that loved us." (Romans 8:37) A captive desires a speedy liberation, so he may not die in exile or suffer lack of food. God says, **"But I am the LORD your God, that divided the sea, whose waves roared. The LORD of hosts is his name." 51:14-15** God would be with them.

"And I have put my words in your mouth, and have covered you in the shadow of my hand, that I may plant the heavens and lay the foundations of the earth, and say to Zion, 'You are my people.'" 51:16 These words are addressed to spiritual Zion, God's faithful remnant. Similar words were spoken to the Lord's Suffering Servant, the Messiah, in Isaiah 49:2. The message of the Christ will be the message of his church, which speaks of "new heavens and a new earth, wherein righteousness dwells" for God's people. (2 Peter 3:13; Rev. 21:1-5)

Awake, awake, stand up, O Jerusalem, which has drunk at the hand of the LORD the cup of his fury. 51:17 Jerusalem is pictured as a drunken woman; the city lay helpless and defenseless. She was drunken, "but not with wine" (v. 21), but with the cup of God's wrath. **There is none to guide her**; only the LORD could save her. **51:18 These two things are come to you ... desolation and destruction** upon the land and the city **and the famine and the sword** upon the people. **51:19**

The LORD says, **"Behold, I have taken out of your hand the cup of trembling, even the dregs of the cup of my fury; you shall no more drink it again. But I will put it into the hand of them that afflict you." 51:22-23** The LORD's wrath would be for Babylon.

Awake, awake, put on your strength, O Zion; put on your beautiful garments, O Jerusalem, the holy city. 52:1 The holy city is the bride of Christ, his church (Rev. 21:9-10; Ephesians 5:25-27). She is clothed with beautiful garments of Christ's righteousness. (Gal. 3:27; 1 Cor. 1:30; Rev. 19:7-8;)

O Jerusalem: loose yourself from the bands of your neck, O captive daughter of Zion. 52:2 Christ can set all mankind free from the spiritual bondage that is symbolized by the captive bands on the neck of the daughter of Zion.

"You have sold yourselves for nothing; and you shall be redeemed without money." 52:3 Christ's "everlasting covenant" provides blessings that cannot be purchased with money. (Isaiah 55:1-3; 1 Peter 1:18-19)

"Therefore my people shall know my name." 52:6 In the new covenant of Christ, "they shall not teach every man his neighbor and every man his brother, saying, 'Know the LORD,' for they shall all know me." (Hebrews 8:6-11)

How beautiful upon the mountains are the feet of him who brings good news, who proclaims peace, who brings glad tidings of good things, who proclaims salvation, who says to Zion, "Your God reigns!" 52:7 NKJV Nahum alluded to this verse in predicting the fall of Nineveh and the kingdom of Assyria. (Nahum 1:15) The Jews would rejoice at the good news decreed by Cyrus that they could return to Jerusalem. But it has a broader fulfillment. This verse is quoted in Romans 10:15 and is applied to the preaching of the gospel of Christ that brings peace, happiness, and salvation. Don Shackelford says, "Just as surely as He overthrew Assyria and Babylon, He will overthrow the spiritual host of wickedness in order to bring about our redemption." [60]

Break forth into joy, sing together, you waste places of Jerusalem, for the LORD has comforted his people, he has redeemed Jerusalem. 52:9 The waste places represent people, fallen sinners, who have been redeemed. Jerusalem represents all those that have been redeemed by the LORD. They are to **sing together** with joy, for the LORD has comforted them as his people.

Depart! Depart! Go out from there. Touch no unclean thing; go out from the midst of her; be clean ... For the LORD will go before you; and the God of Israel will be your rear guard. 52:11, 12 NKJV As the Jews left Babylon, they were not to take with them the unclean things of Babylon. Paul refers to this verse as he tells us to cleanse ourselves from all filthiness. (2 Cor. 6:17 – 7:1)

Behold. my servant shall deal prudently, he shall be exalted and extolled. 52:13 The prophet now turns our attention to the Messiah, who is first mentioned as the LORD's elect servant in 42:1. Jesus said, "The Son of man came not to be ministered unto, but to minister, and to give his life a ransom for many." (Matthew 20:28) Because the Messiah would act wisely and prosper, he would be exalted to the throne of God (Acts 2:33) and be praised for his work of redemption.

As many were astonished at you—his appearance was so marred, beyond human semblance. 52:14 ESV When Jerusalem and the temple were destroyed, many could not believe it; they thought God would never allow

---

[60] Shackelford, Ibid., p. 530

that to happen. When Jesus was crucified, his followers were shocked. How could Jesus, who had shown so much power, be so humiliated! His head was covered with blood from the crown of thorns. His body was mutilated by the scourging. (cf. 50:6) Crucifixion was the most agonizing death ever devised by man.

So shall he sprinkle many nations. 52:15 Under the Law of Moses, the sprinkling of blood was for cleansing and consecration. (Lev. 4:1-6) Through his suffering and death, Christ would bring the cleansing of sinners and their dedication to the LORD. The closing verses of Isaiah 52 serve as an introduction to the suffering servant.

Who has believed our report? 53:1 This rhetorical question indicates his report would not be believed. In predicting the virgin birth of Christ, Isaiah had said his name would be Immanuel, meaning "God with us." (7:14; Matthew 1:23) He also had said there would be the voice crying in the wilderness, "Prepare the way of the LORD (Yahweh); make straight in the desert a highway for our God." But when the Christ came into the world, he was accused of blasphemy for saying he was the Christ, the Son of God. (Matthew 26:62-66) Paul stated, "They have not all obeyed the gospel. For Isaiah says, 'Lord, who has believed our report?'" (Romans 10:16) Isaiah predicted that many would not believe it. They were not looking for the Messiah described by Isaiah, but they were desiring an earthly king like David or Solomon.

For he shall grow up before him as a tender plant, and as a root out of dry ground; he has no form or comeliness; and when we shall see him, there is no beauty that we should desire him. 53:2 In Isaiah 11:1, the prophet calls the Messiah a Branch that would grow out of the roots of Jesse. There had been no king of

David's lineage since the Babylonian exile. Also, Jesus grew up in Nazareth, an obscure town in Galilee. When Nathanael first heard about Jesus, he asked, "Can there any good thing come out of Nazareth?" (John 1:46) People would not be attracted to him by his physical appearance. He would appear to be an ordinary man.

He is despised and rejected of men; a man of sorrows and acquainted with grief. 53:3 Isaiah predicted the rejection of Jesus. "He came to his own, and his own received him not." (John 1:11) The Jewish rulers called him a "Samaritan" (John 8:48) and "Beelzebub," the ruler of the demons (Matthew 10:25; Luke 11:15). Jesus was "grieved" by the hardness of men's hearts. (Mark 3:5) He said, "My soul is exceedingly sorrowful." (Matthew 26:38)

Surely, he has borne our griefs and carried our sorrows: yet we did esteem him stricken, smitten of God, and afflicted. 53:4 While Jesus was suffering physical pain and mental anguish for our sins, the people thought that God was punishing him for his own sins. During his trial they said he was guilty of blasphemy, and they mocked him as he hung on the cross. Homer Hailey observes, "Little did the people realize that He was being subjected to such indignities for their sins, not His own." [61]

But he was wounded for our transgressions, he was bruised for our iniquities; the chastisement of our peace was upon him, and with his stripes we are healed. 53:5 Christ suffered for our sins, and his atoning sacrifice made possible our peace with God and our spiritual healing. The Holy Spirit, who was inspiring Isaiah's words was so certain of what would be done that He spoke of these future events in the past tense, **he was wounded.** "God ... calls those things which are not as

---

[61] Homer Hailey, *A Commentary on Isaiah*, p. 438

though they were." (Romans 4:17) Homer Hailey states, "Instead of **wounded**, several commentators (including Delitzsch and Young) suggest **pierced**, which more accurately reflects what is said in other passages. Not only were the Servant's hands and feet pierced with nails (Ps. 22:16) and His side pierced with a spear (John 19:34), but Zechariah prophesied (12:10) that one day the inhabitants of Jerusalem would look unto Him whom they had pierced (John 19:37). **He was bruised**, a strong word meaning 'to crush,' which emphasizes the emotional and spiritual suffering of the Servant as He became sin on our behalf ... The punishment for our transgressions and iniquities which had broken the unity, the relationship, between man and God, was laid upon the Servant; **and with His stripes we are healed**, restored to complete harmony with God. In bearing the guilt of man's sins, the Servant also bore the punishment for them ... separation from God." [62] Psalm 22:1-18 predicts this separation and his crucifixion.

All we like sheep have gone astray; we have turned everyone to his own way; and the LORD** has laid on him the iniquity of us all. 53:6** All of us have strayed from the L**ORD**, our Shepherd. (Psalm 23) And like a sheep seeking out greener pastures on his own, each one of us, from time to time, has rejected God's way for our own way. The punishment for our failure to follow our Shepherd has been laid on the Suffering Servant.

He was oppressed, and he was afflicted, yet he opened not his mouth. He is brought as a lamb to the slaughter, and as a sheep before her shearers is dumb, so he opens not his mouth. 53:7 His sacrifice for our sins is described as a lamb being led to the slaughter. Men are compared to sheep, and Christ was made in the likeness of men (Philippians 2:5-7). It was necessary for

---

[62] Hailey, Ibid., pp. 438-439

Christ to have a human body to be the sacrifice for our sins. (Hebrews 10:4-10) This is the first time in Scripture that the Christ is described as a lamb. As a lamb goes quietly to the slaughter, Jesus remained silent many times during his trials before the Sanhedrin (Matthew 26:59-63), before Pilate (Matthew 27:12-14), and before Herod (Luke 23:9).

He was taken from prison and from judgment; and who shall declare his generation? For he was cut off out of the land of the living. 53:8 Jesus was arrested by the chief priests, and the Sanhedrin judged him guilty of blasphemy and deserving of death. (Matthew 26:47-66) Desiring to crucify Jesus, they took him to be judged by Pilate the governor, accusing him of perverting the nation and claiming to be a king. (Luke 23:1-2) After examining Jesus, the governor said, "I have found no fault in this man touching those things whereof you accuse him." (Luke 23:14) However, because of the insistence of the people and the chief priests, he granted that Jesus be crucified. (Luke 23:20-24) Isaiah clearly predicted that the Suffering Servant, the Christ, would be killed, "cut off out of the land of the living."

For the transgression of my people, he was stricken. 53:8 The Servant would be killed because God's people had rebelled. Shackelford says, "The word 'transgression' is better translated 'rebellion.' All the while, 'his generation' would not understand the significance of His atoning sacrifice." [63]

He was assigned a grave with the wicked, and with the rich in his death; though he had done no violence, nor was any deceit in his mouth. 53:9 [NIV] This prophecy is amazing in its details! Graves were prepared for Jesus and for the two criminals that were crucified with him, so they made his grave with the wicked. But a rich man, Joseph

---

[63] Don Shackelford, *Truth for Today Commentary, Isaiah*, p. 540

of Arimathea, was given permission by Pilate to bury the body of Jesus in his own new tomb. (Matthew 27:57-60) Jesus was not deserving of death, as the Sanhedrin had judged him. He had not been guilty of violence or deceit. He had lived a perfectly sinless life and had told the truth.

Yet it pleased the LORD to bruise him; he has put him to grief. When you shall make his soul an offering for sin, he shall see his seed, he shall prolong his days, and the pleasure of the LORD shall prosper in his hand. 53:10 The LORD was pleased that the Messiah provided salvation for lost mankind, even though it put him to grief. (John 3:16) In addition to the physical suffering and death of his body, Christ would make **"his soul an offering for sin."** God "made him to be sin for us, who knew no sin; that we might be made the righteousness of God in him." (2 Cor. 5:21) During three hours of darkness on the cross, Jesus was bearing our sins. (Mark 15:33; 1 Pet. 2:24) Sin causes separation from God. (Isaiah 59:1-2). When the darkness ended, Jesus cried out with a loud voice, "My God, my God, why have you forsaken me?" (Mark 5:34) He had fulfilled Psalm 22:1-22 and Isaiah's prophecy.

He shall see the travail of his soul and shall be satisfied. 53:11 Because his Servant was willing to make this atoning sacrifice, the LORD would **"prolong his days"** by raising him from the dead. The Christ **"shall see his seed"** – the children of God by faith (Galatians 3:26-29); he would bring "many sons to glory" according to Hebrews 2:9-10. **"The pleasure of the LORD"** refers to God's "eternal purpose which he purposed in Christ Jesus our Lord" (Ephesians 3:11), and it **"shall prosper in his hand"** because in him "we have boldness and access with confidence by the faith of him." (Ephesians 3:12)

By his knowledge shall my righteous Servant justify many; for he shall bear their iniquities. 53:11 Many will be forgiven and have a right relationship with God by their knowing Christ and his atoning sacrifice. Jesus prayed to the heavenly Father, saying, "And this is life eternal, that they might know you the only true God and Jesus Christ, whom you have sent." (John 17:3) God desires everyone to "come to the knowledge of the truth." (1 Timothy 2:3-4) Christ brings salvation! He is God's Righteous Servant.

Therefore, I will divide him a portion with the great, and he shall divide the spoil with the strong, because he has poured out his soul unto death, and he was numbered with the transgressors, and made intercession for the transgressors. 53:12 Christ proved his victory over Satan. God raised Jesus from the dead and gave him all power in heaven and on earth. (Matthew 28:18) "As the children are partakers of flesh and blood, he also himself likewise took part of the same, that through death he might destroy him that had the power of death, that is, the devil; and deliver them who through fear of death were all their lifetime subject to bondage." (Hebrews 2:14-15) "For he must reign till he has put all enemies under his feet. The last enemy to be destroyed is death." (1 Cor. 15:25-26) Our victory is in Jesus Christ. Through him, we have the promise of an eternal inheritance. (Hebrews 9:14-15) We have this hope, because he was willing to "pour out his soul unto death" – separation from God. He bore our sins on the cross; he was numbered among the transgressors. He died in our place as our sin offering.

Review Questions on Isaiah 49 - 53

1. Who is the Lord's Servant in 49-53? _____

2. "He has made my mouth like a _____ _____." 49:2

3. "The day of salvation" is the _____. 49:8

4. Christ would be given "as a _____." 49:8

5. The Servant says, "I offered my _____ to those who beat me, my _____ to those who pulled out my beard; I did not hide my face from _____ and _____." 50:6 NIV

6. "For the Lord GOD will _____ me; therefore … I shall not be ashamed." 50:7

7. "The _____ will vanish away … but my _____ shall be forever." 51:6

8. "Fear not the _____ of men, neither be afraid of their _____." 51:7

9. The _____ of the LORD shall return and come with _____ unto Zion. 51:11

10. Jerusalem is to put on _____ garments. 52:1

11. "How beautiful upon the mountain are the feet of him who brings _____ _____, who proclaims _____!" 52:7

12. The Servant's appearance was so _____ beyond human semblance. 52:14 ᴱˢⱽ

13. The Servant would grow up "as a tender _____ and as a root out of _____ ground." 53:2

14. Jesus did not attract others by his _____.

15. "He is _____ and _____ of men." 53:3

16. "Surely he has borne our griefs and carried our _____ yet we did esteem him stricken, smitten of _____."

17. "But he was wounded for our _____, he was bruised for our _____; the chastisement of our _____ was upon him, and with his _____ we are healed." 53:5

18. "All we like _____ have gone astray; we have turned every one to his own _____." 53:6

19. "He is brought as a _____ to the slaughter." 53:7

20. "He was assigned a grave with the _____, and with the _____ in his death." 53:9 ᴺᴵⱽ

21. The Lord "shall prolong his days" by _____ him from the _____. 53:10

The Covenant of Peace
Isaiah 54 – 57

The covenant of peace is made possible by the suffering Servant's atoning sacrifice. "My kindness shall not depart from you, neither shall **the covenant of my peace** be removed," says the LORD. (54:10) He promises, "I will make **an everlasting covenant** with you, even the sure mercies of David." (55:3) These promises are fulfilled in the new covenant of Christ. "Therefore, being justified by faith, we have **peace** through our Lord Jesus Christ." (Romans 5:1)

"Sing, O barren, you that did not bear; break forth into singing, and cry aloud, you that did not travail with child: for more are the children of the desolate than the children of the married wife," says the LORD. 54:1 This verse is quoted in Galatians 4:21-31 to show that Abraham's wife Sarah and her handmaid Hagar represent two covenants: Hagar is the old covenant dependent upon the flesh, and Sarah is the new covenant dependent upon "the promise." Sarah had no children until Isaac, "the child of promise," was born. (Gen. 18) God promised Abraham that in his seed all nations of the earth would be blessed (Genesis 22:18); the blessing would be the forgiveness of sins. (Acts 3:25-26) Israel was "the married wife" of the LORD under the old covenant. (Jer. 3:8) Sarah is "the desolate" mother who was promised children – including the Gentiles who were at that time "aliens from the commonwealth of Israel." (Eph. 2:11-13) In the new covenant those of all nations are now "children of promise, as Isaac was." (Gal. 4:28) Abraham's children of promise will be far greater in number than his physical offspring. (Gal. 3:7-9, 26-29)

Hagar is the law from Mount Sinai "which gives birth to bondage." Those of the new covenant are to "sing" praises to the LORD because they are now the "children of promise."

"Enlarge the place of your tent." 54:2 Abraham would need a larger dwelling place, because his spiritual family would include those of all nations who are of faith in Christ, whose "dominion shall be from sea to sea ... even to the ends of the earth." (Zechariah 9:10) A **tent** describes our temporary dwelling place. Like Abraham, we are looking for "a city which has foundations whose builder and maker is God." (Hebrews 11:10)

"For you shall break forth to the right hand and on the left, and your seed shall inherit the Gentiles." 54:3 Abraham's seed would include the Gentiles, those of other nations. The apostle Paul states in Galatians 3:7-8, "They which are of faith, the same are the children of Abraham. And the Scripture foreseeing that God would justify the heathen through faith, preached beforehand the gospel unto Abraham, saying, 'In you shall all nations be blessed.'" And Galatians 3:28 concludes, "There is neither Jew nor Greek ... for you are all one in Christ Jesus. And if you are Christ's, then you are Abraham's seed, and heirs according to the promise." In giving the great commission Jesus said, "Go you therefore and teach all nations." (Matthew 28:18-20)

"Fear not; for you shall not be ashamed. For your Maker is your husband; the LORD of hosts is his name, and your Redeemer the Holy One of Israel, the God of the whole earth." 54:4, 5 Christ would build his church; He would be her Maker. (Matthew 16:18) He would redeem the church with his blood. (Ephesians 1:7; Acts 20:28) "Christ also loved the church and gave Himself for her, that he might sanctify and cleanse her with the washing of water by the word, that He might present her to Himself a glorious church, not having spot or wrinkle or any such thing, but that she should be holy and without blemish." ᴺᴷᴶⱽ (Eph. 5:25-27) His church will have no reason to fear or be ashamed, for Christ is her husband. (Ephesians 5:29-32)

"For a moment I have forsaken you; but with great mercies I will gather you. In a little wrath I hid my face from you for a moment; but with everlasting kindness I will have mercy on you," says the LORD your redeemer. 54:7-8 The rejection and punishment of his people in the past is brief when compared with his everlasting compassion and mercy for the redeemed.

"For the mountains shall depart and the hills be removed, but my kindness shall not depart from you, neither shall the covenant of my peace be removed," says the LORD, who has mercy on you. 54:10 The covenant of peace is the new covenant of Christ. (Jeremiah 31:31-34; Hebrews 8:6-13) Homer Hailey said, "This promise is not made to national Israel or physical Jerusalem, for both experienced the vent of His indignation from soon after the return from exile until the destruction by the Romans. Rather, the promise is made to spiritual Israel. It does not mean that she will not be severely tested. What it does mean is that though she might be unmercifully persecuted ... the true spiritual Zion and Jerusalem (the church) will never be the object of God's wrath."[64] God's covenant of peace is an everlasting covenant (Hebrews 13:20-21), and it is like the everlasting covenant that God made with Noah in Genesis 9:11-16, promising never to destroy the whole earth again with water. **54:9**

---

[64] Homer Hailey, *A Commentary on Isaiah*, p. 447

"O you afflicted, tossed with tempest and not comforted, I will lay your stones with fair colors, and lay your foundations with sapphires." 54:11 The heavenly New Jerusalem in Revelation 21 is described with similar figurative language. Don Shackelford says, "Earthly cities like Babylon were beautiful but temporary. The city of God is everlasting." [65]

"And all your children shall be taught of the LORD, and great shall be the peace of your children." 54:13 In explaining how God draws people by the Scriptures, Jesus quoted Isaiah. He said, "No man can come to me, except the Father which has sent me draws him, and I will raise him up at the last day. It is written in the prophets, **'And they shall all be taught of God.'** Every man therefore that has heard and has learned of the Father comes to me." (John 6:44-45). Obeying the teachings of God brings peace.

"In righteousness you shall be established ... for you shall not fear." 54:14 The Lord makes us righteous by the gospel of Christ, "for therein the righteousness of God is revealed from faith to faith; as it is written, 'The just shall live by faith.'" (Romans 1:16-17) Hebrews 13:6 promises, "We may boldly say, 'The LORD is my helper; I will not fear. What can man do to me?'" NKJV

"No weapon that is formed against you shall prosper; and every tongue that shall rise against you in judgment you shall condemn. This is the heritage of the servants of the LORD, and their righteousness is of me," says the LORD. 54:17 Hailey explains, "No weapon that is formed against His city can defeat or destroy her. Furthermore, every tongue that accuses her shall be condemned by the truth abiding in His people. This is assurance of divine protection and victory over

---

[65] Shackelford, Ibid., p. 549

their enemies is a permanent possession of God's servants." [66] Don Shackelford states, "Our righteousness is in reality His righteousness ... Up to this point, Isaiah's prophecy has spoken of the 'servant' (singular); but from this point forward, the book speaks 'servants' (plural) as God's people. This refers to both the redeemed of Israel and spiritual Israel, the church." [67]

"Ho! Everyone that thirsts, come to the waters; and he that has no money, come, buy, and eat. Yes, come, buy wine and milk without money and without price." 55:1 After promising the blessings in chapter 54, Israel is invited to accept these blessings in chapter 55. **Ho!** draws attention to the LORD's invitation. **Come to the waters,** the water of life (Rev. 21:6) that proceed from the throne of God (Rev. 22:1). **He that has no money come** describes the spiritual poverty of one invited to come. The provisions being offered are **without money and without cost.** Romans 6:23 says, "The free gift of God is eternal life in Christ Jesus our Lord." NASB He paid for our redemption with his blood. (Ephesians 1:7). "For by grace you are saved through faith; and that not of yourselves, it is the gift of God." (Ephesians 2:8)

"Why do you spend money for that which is not bread and your labor for that which satisfies not?" 55:2 Physical food never satisfies for long; we get hungry again. And it cannot satisfy our spiritual hunger—our greatest need. When tempted Jesus answered Satan, "It is written, 'Man shall not live by bread alone, but by every word that proceeds from the mouth of God.'" (Matthew 4:4) And he instructed in John 6:27, "Do not labor for the food which perishes, but for the food which endures to everlasting life, which the Son of Man will give you." NKJV

---

[66] Hailey, Ibid., p. 451
[67] Shackelford, Ibid., p. 550

"Incline your ear and come to me. Hear, and your soul shall live." 55:3 While declaring that he is "the bread of life," Jesus explained, "The words that I speak unto you, they are spirit, and they are life." (John 6:63) The LORD is speaking to the individual sinner.

"And I will make an everlasting covenant with you, even the sure mercies of David. Behold, I have given him for a witness to the people." 55:3-4 The LORD promised David in 2 Samuel 7:8-16 that he would set up his seed after him and establish the throne of his kingdom forever. Later, David committed adultery with Bathsheba. (2 Sam. 11:1-5) To cover his sin, David made sure that her husband was killed in battle, and he married her. The punishment for adultery under the Law was death. (Leviticus 20:10) However, when David repented and confessed his sins, God forgave him; and David did not die. (2 Samuel 12:1-13) David then wrote Psalm 51 in which he confesses his sins and Psalm 32 in which he rejoices in the LORD's mercy. **The sure mercies of David** would be offered in the everlasting covenant, and David would be given "for a witness to the people." The New Testament is the **everlasting covenant**. In Acts 13:22, David is described as a man after God's "own heart" who would fulfill all of God's will. God desires all of us to repent. (Acts 17:30; 2 Peter 3:9) When David sinned, he truly repented and accepted the consequences; and God gave him mercy. In Acts 13:34, Paul quotes Isaiah 55:3, **"I will give you the sure mercies of David."** Paul concludes in verses 38-39 that through Jesus Christ "is preached unto you the forgiveness of sins; and by him all that believe are justified from all things, from which you could not be justified by the Law of Moses." In Romans 4:6-7, Paul quotes Psalm 32, saying, "Even as David also describes the blessedness of the man unto whom God imputes righteousness without works, saying, 'Blessed are they whose iniquities are forgiven, and whose sins are covered.'" David serves as an example of true repentance and of God's mercy that would be made possible through Jesus Christ, the seed of David who would be a leader and commander to the people.

"Behold, you shall call a nation that you know not, and nations that knew not you shall run to you because of the LORD your God." 55:5 Christ would call a nation into being that was previously unknown. It will be the church, "a holy nation" that will be "called" out of darkness into God's marvelous light. (1 Peter 2:9) Homer Hailey explains, "By means of the gospel, this nation will be called from among 'the nations' (Matthew 28:18-20; Mark 16:15-16). People who have not known Him will hasten unto Him; they will flow unto God's holy mountain from which Messiah will reign (2:2-3)." [68]

Seek the LORD while he may be found, call upon him while he is near. 55:6 To seek the LORD is to make an effort to know him and to obey his will. God rewards "those who diligently seek him." (Hebrews 11:6) Jesus promises, "Seek, and you shall find." (Matthew 7:7) Paul urges his hearers to "seek the Lord" and "find him," because "he is not far from every one of us." (Acts 17:27) But we must seek him **while he may be found**, because we may not have the opportunity later. Now is the time to seek the LORD.

Let the wicked forsake his way, and the unrighteous man his thoughts; and let him return unto the LORD, and he will have mercy upon him; and to our God, for he will abundantly pardon. 55:7 The sinner is to renounce his sinful way of living and his ungodly thoughts. Repentance requires forsaking our sins and returning to God in obedience to his will. The

---

[68] Hailey, Ibid., p. 454

person who repents will receive mercy from God and complete forgiveness of his sins.

"**For my thoughts are not your thoughts, neither your ways my ways,**" says the LORD. "**For as the heavens are higher than the earth, so are my ways higher than your ways, and my thoughts than your thoughts.**" **55:8-9** Proverbs 14:12 warns, "There is a way that seems right to a man, but its end is the way of death." NKJV There's the danger of elevating our own ways and thoughts while ignoring God's will. When God tells us of his grace, as he does in verse 7, we may respond incorrectly in two ways. We may not confess our sins, or we may not accept God's grace. On one hand, we may think we are good enough without God's forgiveness; and on the other hand, we may think that our sins are so great they cannot be forgiven.

"**For as the rain comes down, and the snow from heaven, and ... waters the earth, and makes it bring forth and bud, that it may give seed to the sower and bread to the eater, so shall my word be that goes forth out of my mouth; it shall not return unto me void, but it shall accomplish that which I please, and it shall prosper in the thing for which I sent it.**" **55:10-11** Homer Hailey makes the following comments: "As the rain and snow accomplish God's purpose in the earth, so His word will fulfill His purpose in the hearts of those who draw near to hear, give heed, and change their ways and thoughts ... When heeded, His word completely changes the life of men, fulfilling God's desires." [69]

"**You shall go out with joy, and be led forth with peace; the mountains and the hills shall break forth before you into singing.**" **55:12** Our receiving the everlasting covenant of Christ will bring to us joy and peace.

---

[69] Hailey, Ibid., 456

The land metaphorically will sing praises to God for his blessings.

"Instead of the thorn shall come up the fir tree, and instead of the brier shall come up the myrtle tree; and it shall be to the LORD for a name, for an everlasting sign that shall not be cut off." 55:13 Briars and thorns came up when God laid waste his vineyard (5:5-6), which figuratively describes of the destruction of earthly Jerusalem. But in the heavenly Jerusalem there will be the fir (or cypress) tree and the myrtle tree—evergreen trees which are symbols of life. At the Feast of Tabernacles, the booths were made of branches from the myrtle tree. (Nehemiah 8:15) Hosea uses the cypress tree as a symbol of the LORD's presence. (Hosea 14:8)

"Keep justice and do righteousness, for My salvation is about to come, and My righteousness to be revealed." 56:1 ^{NKJV} The righteousness of God is revealed in the gospel of Christ, which is God's power to save us. (Romans 1:16-17) Having been justified by faith in our Lord Jesus Christ (Romans 5:1), we are to be servants of righteousness unto holiness. (Romans 6:18-19)

"Blessed is the man ... that keeps the Sabbath from polluting it, and keeps his hand from doing any evil." 56:2 The Jews were commanded, "Remember the Sabbath, to keep it holy." (Ex. 20:8) God would bless the person that properly observed the Sabbath and the Law given to Israel at Mount. Sinai. The Sabbath observance reminded Israel of God's power in the creation (Genesis 2:3) and in their deliverance from their bondage in Egypt. (Deuteronomy 5:15) One who had faithfully observed the Law of Moses would faithfully observe the new covenant of Christ. (Matthew 5:19; James 1:25; 2:12)

"**Neither let the son of the stranger that has joined himself to the** L**ORD** **speak saying, 'The** L**ORD** **has utterly separated me from his people'; nor let the eunuch say, 'I am a dry tree.'" 56:3** Those who previously had been excluded under the Law of Moses are given hope in verses 3-8. The first group was the foreigners who had been converted from paganism to the Jewish religion to serve the true God, and the second group was the eunuchs. (Deuteronomy 23:1). Although the proselyte could offer sacrifices (Num. 15:14) and pray toward the temple (1 Kings 8:41-43), he was separated from the assembly. "Herod's temple provided a Court of the Gentiles; if they ventured beyond it, however, they were liable to the death penalty." [70] But the proselyte was not totally separated from God's people. The Ethiopian eunuch had come to worship God in Jerusalem. (Acts 8:27) However, after his baptism into Christ, "he went on his way rejoicing" (Acts 8:39), because we are now "all one in Christ Jesus." (Galatians 3:26-28)

"I will give them an everlasting name." 56:5 This promise is messianic. With the coming of Christ, all barriers were removed for the faithful proselytes and eunuchs. (Eph. 2:14-15; 3:14-15) They were given the name "Christian." (Isaiah 62:2; Acts 11:1-26)

"Also, the sons of the stranger that join themselves to the L**ORD****, to serve him … even them I will bring to my holy mountain." 56:6-7** Many Gentiles believed in the LORD after the Jews returned to Jerusalem, and they came to Mount Zion to worship. **"My house shall be called a house of prayer for all people." 56:7** Jesus quoted this verse in Matthew 21:13. God-fearing Gentiles worshiped in the Jewish synagogues where Paul preached. (Acts 13:16, 43) This prophecy finds its complete fulfillment in the church, the heavenly Mount

---

[70] Hailey, Ibid., p. 459

Zion. (Isaiah 2:2-3; Hebrews 12:22-24) We can see it being fulfilled in the book of Acts. The Ethiopian eunuch was reading Isaiah 53:7-8. (Acts 8:30-32) Cornelius was a devout Gentile who prayed to God always. (Acts 10:1-2)

The Lord GOD, who gathers the outcasts of Israel, says, "Yet I will gather others to him besides those that are gathered unto him." 56:8 Jesus said, "Other sheep I have which are not of this fold; them also I must bring, and they shall hear my voice; and there shall be one flock and one shepherd." (John 10:16). This gathering takes place in Christ and his church. (Ephesians 1:10, 22-23)

All you beasts of the field, come and devour, all you beasts in the forest. 56:9 God's people, Israel, were cast out and their kingdoms were devoured by the Assyrians and the Chaldeans, who were like hungry, ferocious beasts. (cf. Hab. 1:6-10) Isaiah was witnessing the devastation by the Assyrians; and he was showing why the "outcasts of Israel" would need to be gathered by the Lord GOD in verse 8.

His watchmen are blind, they are ignorant; they are all dumb dogs, they cannot bark; sleeping, lying down, loving to slumber. Yes, they are greedy dogs which can never have enough. ... They all look to their own way, everyone for his gain. 56:10-11 The leaders of God's people were failing to see the dangers confronting them because of their sins. They were not warning their people. They were complacent and greedily looking out for their own interests. They were like lazy dogs that don't bark when an intruder comes, because their only interest is sleep and more food. Also, their leaders were not seeing things clearly because they were given to wine and strong drink, as they lived in luxury. **56:12**

The righteous perishes, and no man lays it to heart; and merciful men are taken away, none considering that the righteous is taken away from the evil to come. He shall enter into peace; they shall rest in their beds. 57:1-2 Josiah, king of Judah, was a righteous man, and he died so that his eyes would not see all the calamity that God would bring on Jerusalem. (2 Kings 22:20) Hailey explains, "The word *perish* can indicate either a violent or natural death ... When the merciful or godly man is taken away, no one considers that his being removed *from the evil to come* upon the nation is actually a blessing for him: he will be spared the calamity. Micah's parallel description of people in the pre-exilic period (Micah 7:2) confirms that this passage does not refer to postexilic conditions. Not only will the righteous man escape the evil which is to come upon the people, but he will also partake of that well-being, wholeness, and completeness for which the soul of the righteous yearns ... he experiences the eternal rest of victory and redemption which the Lord intends for His people (Hebrews 4:9; cf. Psalm 95:11). In the light of the context, *beds* apparently signify the resting place of the deceased, as when David said, 'If I make my bed in Sheol, behold, thou art there' (Psalm 139:8)." [71] The righteous person enters the peace that is made possible by the new covenant of peace.

"But draw near, you sons of the sorceress, the seed of the adulterer and the whore." 57:3 The LORD is now calling the wicked into judgment. They were followers of **a sorceress**, one that sought supernatural information from demonic spirits. In Exodus 22:18, the Law of Moses stated, "You shall not permit a sorceress to live." NKJV The **adulterer** and the **whore** refer to idolatry, including unlawful sexual relations, which were a part of Baal worship. The wicked were unfaithful to God. That's spiritual adultery.

---

[71] Hailey, Ibid., p. 463

"**Whom do you ridicule? Against whom do you make a wide mouth and stick out the tongue?" 57:4** NKJV When one mocks and scorns a righteous person, he is actually ridiculing the Lord God. **"Are you not children of transgression, a seed of falsehood, inflaming yourselves with idols under every green tree, slaying the children in the valleys under the clefts of the rocks?" 57:4-5** In the worship of idols, they stirred up their lusts and committed sexual immorality, and then they offered the babies of their illicit unions as sacrifices to the Baals in the Valley of Hinnom. (2 Chronicles 28:1-3) Homer Hailey says that **verses 5-12** "are a graphic description of the idolatry which was strongly condemned before the exile. There are no records of such practices after the return from Babylon." [72]

"He that puts his trust in me shall possess the land and shall inherit my holy mountain ... Prepare the way, take up the stumbling block out of the way of my people." 57:13-14 The LORD is referring to the Highway of Holiness, that is described in 35:8-10. Walking in the way of holiness, one will never fall. (2 Peter 1:3-10)

For thus says the high and lofty One that inhabits eternity, whose name is Holy: "I dwell in the high and holy place, with him also that is of a contrite and humble spirit, to revive the spirit of the humble, and to revive the heart of the contrite ones." 57:15 The eternal Lord God is above all of his creation. He is the only one who can bring peace to the humble, because he alone is perfectly **holy** in his being; he is set-apart from all wickedness. Heaven is his dwelling place, **the high and holy place**. Yet he is willing to share Heaven with those who have a humble, contrite heart—those who will repent of their sins. We are reminded of the vision in 6:1 when Isaiah was called to be a prophet. David said in

---

[72] Hailey, Ibid, p. 464

Psalm 138:6, "Though the LORD is on high, yet he has respect to the lowly." James exhorts, "Humble yourselves in the sight of the Lord, and he shall lift you up." (James 4:10)

"For I will not contend forever, nor will I always be angry." 57:16 ᴺᴷᴶⱽ God will not pour out his wrath upon the wickedness of Israel forever. His judgment is followed by mercy for those that repent. His wrath is tempered by his love.

"Peace, peace to him that is far off and to him that is near," says the LORD, "And I will heal him." 57:19 The apostle Paul applied this verse to our Lord Jesus Christ, saying that he "came and preached peace to you which were afar off and to them that were near." (Ephesians 2:17) He is called "The Prince of Peace" in Isaiah 9:6. He gives the greatest peace of all. With his stripes of suffering, he can heal our sinful condition. (Isaiah 53:5) The covenant of peace has been the theme of chapters 54-57.

"But the wicked are like the troubled sea, when it cannot rest, whose waters cast up mire and dirt." 57:20 There is much unrest in the world. Greed, jealousy, hatred, addictions, and despair keep people in a constant turmoil. Broken lives and ugly filth are everywhere. However, God can restore those who turn to him in humble repentance.

"There is no peace," says my God, "to the wicked." 57:21 This chapter closes with the same words that closed chapter 48.

Review Questions on Isaiah 54 – 57

1. "The Covenant of _____" is in Isaiah 54-57.

2. "The children of the desolate" in Isaiah 54:1 are the children of _____, according to Galatians 4:28.

3. "For your Maker is your _____, the LORD."

4. "My _____ shall not depart from you, neither shall the covenant of my _____ be removed." 54:10

5. Jerusalem's children shall be _____ by the Lord. 54:13

6. "In _____ you shall be established." 54:14

7. "No _____ that is formed against you shall prosper, and every _____ which rises against you in judgment you shall condemn." 54:17

8. "Everyone who _____, come to the _____, and you who have no _____, come, buy and eat." 55:1

9. "I will make an _____ covenant with you." 55:3

10. "_____ the LORD while he may be found, _____ upon him while he is near." 55:6

11. "Let the wicked forsake his _____, and the unrighteous man his _____." 55:7

12. "Let him _____ unto the LORD, and he will have _____ on him; and to our God, for he will abundantly _____." 55:7

13. "For my _____ are not your _____, nor your _____ my _____," says the LORD.

14. "So shall my _____ be that goes forth out of my mouth; it shall not return unto me _____." 55:11

15. "My _____ is about to come." 56:1 NKJV

16. "I will bring them to my holy _____." 56:7

17. One who mocks a righteous person is actually ridiculing _____. 57:4

18. "Thus says the high and lofty One that inhabits _____, whose name is _____: 'I dwell in the high and holy place with him also that is of a _____ and _____ spirit.'" 57:15

19. "Peace, peace to him that is _____ _____ and to him who is _____." 57:19 "But the wicked are like a troubled _____, when it cannot rest, whose _____ cast up mire and dirt." 57:20

20. "There is no _____," says my God, "for the wicked." 57:21

The Glorious Future

Isaiah 58 – 66

God's people must be made aware of their sins before they can be restored by the LORD and receive his blessings. Isaiah points out their sins in chapter 58. Their sins have separated them from God, but a Redeemer will come. (Isaiah 59) The glory of the LORD will come upon spiritual Zion, and the redeemed of all nations shall inherit a land where there is no sun or moon, for the LORD will be their "everlasting light." (Isaiah 60) The Messiah would declare the good news of salvation. Spiritual Zion, the redeemed, will be clothed with "the robe of righteousness." (Isaiah 61) New Jerusalem, the saved of all nations, "shall be called by a new name." (Isaiah 62) The Messiah alone will conquer Satan, by himself. (Isaiah 63) Isaiah confesses that "all our righteous acts are like filthy rags," and he prays for mercy in chapter 64. A new spiritual nation will replace the physical nation of Israel and will inherit new heavens and a new earth. (Isaiah 65) God is on his throne in heaven. He punishes the hypocrites and unbelievers and gives glory and peace to his people. (Isaiah 66)

"Lift up your voice like a trumpet and show my people their transgression, and the house of Jacob their sins." 58:1 Their sins involved religious fasting and the Sabbath. The people were religious. They pretended to be seeking the LORD, but they were insincere. **58:2-3**

Behold, on the day of your fast, you seek your own pleasure and oppress all your workers. Behold, you fast only to quarrel and to fight. 58:3b, 4 ᴱˢⱽ While they fasted, they were thinking only about their businesses and how they might exploit others.

Is it such a fast that I have chosen, a day for a man to afflict his soul? 58:5 The only fast commanded by the law was on the Day of Atonement. (Leviticus 23:26-32) **Is not this the fast I have chosen: to loose the bands of wickedness and to let the oppressed go free? 58:6** The fast God had chosen was to be a time of prayer and humble confession of sins with helping the oppressed.

Then shall your light break forth as morning, and your health shall spring forth speedily; and your righteousness shall go before you; the glory of the LORD shall be your rear guard. Then shall you call, and the LORD shall answer. 58:8-9 When they humbled themselves in genuine repentance and love for God and for others, God would hear their prayers and bless them.

"If you turn away ... from doing your pleasure on my holy day; and call the Sabbath a delight, ... then shall you delight yourself in the LORD; and I will cause you to ride upon the high places of the earth and feed you with the heritage of Jacob." 58:13-14 The LORD had given the Sabbath to Israel (Ex. 16:29) as a sign of the covenant God had made with that nation (Ex. 31:15); but they had failed to properly observe the Sabbath. We show by our actions, as well as our words, that we truly delight in the Lord.

Behold, the LORD's hand is not shortened that it cannot save; neither his ear heavy that it cannot hear. But your iniquities have separated between you and your God, and your sins have hidden his face from you, that he will not hear. 59:1-2 Our sins separate us from God. The prophet describes their sins in verses 3-7, which included speaking lies and shedding innocent blood. Their wicked deeds are described as a **cockatrice**, a poisonous snake. **"The way of peace they know not." 59:8** Without God, there is no peace. (Ephesians 2:11-18)

Our transgressions are multiplied before you, and our sins testify against us. 59:12 In their sins, they were groping in darkness like the blind in desolate places. Truth is nowhere to be found, and whoever shuns evil becomes a prey. **The LORD looked and was displeased that there was no justice. 59:15** NIV The LORD saw that there was no man to intercede for those who were seeking the truth and righteousness and were being mistreated. Therefore, **his arm brought salvation** to him that was a victim of the wicked, and **his righteousness** sustained him. God's **arm** is a metaphor of his power to save. (52:10) The LORD put on **righteousness as a breastplate and a helmet of salvation. 59:16-17** The breastplate and helmet of the Christian's armor is described in this same way. (Eph. 6:10-17)

"And the Redeemer shall come to Zion, and unto them that turn from transgression in Jacob," says the LORD. "As for me, this is my covenant with them," says the LORD. "My Spirit that is upon you and my words which I have put in your mouth shall not depart out of your mouth, nor out of the mouth of your seed," says the LORD, "from henceforth and forever." 59:20-21 This prophecy is applied to Christ in Romans 11:26-27. And Isaiah had said, "Out of **Zion** shall go forth the law, and the word of the LORD from Jerusalem." (2:3) The LORD promised in Isaiah 55:3, "I will make **an everlasting covenant** with you, even the sure mercies of David." The old covenant of Moses was temporary and would be replaced by the new covenant of Christ, which will be everlasting. (Jer. 31:31-34) In the new covenant, God promises, "Their sins and their iniquities I will remember no more." (cf. Hebrews 8:7-12) Jesus Christ is our Redeemer. "The Spirit of the LORD" was upon Jesus; he was anointed to preach the gospel. (Luke 4:18-21) The Father put his words in the mouth of Jesus, and he spoke them. (John 12:49-50) His seed, Christians, are to speak the words of the gospel. (1 Peter 4:11, Mark 16:15)

Arise, shine; for your light has come! And the glory of the LORD is risen upon you. 60:1 Christ "has brought life and immortality to light through the gospel." (2 Tim. 1:10) In a world of spiritual darkness, Christ has come to give us spiritual light and glory. (John 1:4-9; 3:19-21) We are to walk in that light. (1 John 1:7)

And the Gentiles shall come to your light. 60:3 When "the mountain of the LORD's house" was established and the law and the word of the LORD went forth from Zion in Jerusalem, all nations would flow unto it, according to Isaiah 2:2-3. The prophet now says, **"Lift up your eyes round about and see: they all gather themselves together; they come to you; your sons shall come from far." 60:4** Among the nations coming to spiritual Zion would be the exiles of Israel and Judah. Isaiah uses figurative language to describe the gathering of the nations to Messiah's light and glory in **60:6-16**.

"And they shall call you, The City of the LORD, The Zion of the Holy One of Israel." 60:14b Those redeemed by the blood of Christ shall be called the New Jerusalem and Zion. **"You shall know that I, the LORD, am your Savior and your Redeemer, the mighty One of Jacob." 60:16**b

"The sun shall be no more your light by day; neither for brightness shall the moon give light unto you, but the LORD shall be to you an everlasting light, and your God your glory." 60:19 The New Jerusalem's greatest blessing will be heaven, where there is "no need of the sun, neither of the moon to shine in it," for the glory of God and the Lamb is the light. "And the nations of them which are saved shall walk in the light of it." ... "And there shall be no night there ... neither light of the sun; for the Lord God gives them light." (Rev. 21:23-24; 22:5) God is our eternal light!

"Your people also shall all be righteous; they shall inherit the land forever ... that I may be glorified." 60:21 All the inhabitants of the New Jerusalem shall be righteous. "There shall by no means enter it anything that defiles or causes an abomination or a lie, but only those who are written in the Lamb's Book of Life." ᴺᴷᴶⱽ (Revelation 21:27) God our Father "has begotten us again unto a living hope by the resurrection of Jesus Christ from the dead, to an inheritance incorruptible, and undefiled, and that fades not away, reserved in heaven for you." (1 Peter 1:3-4) Jesus Christ is coming again for God "to be glorified in his saints, and to be admired in all them that believe." (2 Thessalonians 1:10) In a prophetic vision, the apostle John saw a great multitude from all nations, clothed with white robes, before the throne in heaven, saying, "Salvation to our God which sits upon the throne and unto the Lamb." (Revelation 7:9-17)

"The Spirit of the Lord God is upon me, because the Lord has anointed me to preach good tidings unto the meek; he has sent me to bind up the brokenhearted, to proclaim liberty to the captives, and the opening of the prison to them that are bound; to proclaim the acceptable year of the Lord." 61:1-2 Jesus read this passage from Isaiah in the synagogue at Nazareth, and then he said, "This day this Scripture is fulfilled in your ears." (Luke 4:15-24) Jesus claimed to be the Servant described by Isaiah. He is called God's Servant in Acts 3:13, 26; 4:27, 30. Jesus preached good news to the meek and to the poor in spirit; he liberated those who were captives of Satan. He came to destroy the devil, who had brought death to mankind, and he delivered "them who through fear of death were all their lifetime subject to bondage." (Heb. 2:14-15) Christ would **"give unto them beauty for ashes, the oil of joy for mourning." 61:3** He will give us a "glorious body" for our earthly body of dust (Philippians 3:21); he will give us joy for our tears.

They will repair the ruined cities, the desolations of many generations. 61:4 But you will be called the priests of the LORD**; you will be spoken of as ministers of our God. 61:6** ^NASB Don Shackelford explains, "The reference is not simply to the rebuilding of Jerusalem after the exile, but also to the building up of spiritual Zion that was to come through the Messiah. In spiritual Zion, there is no special priesthood. Those who enter into the covenant —both Jews and Gentiles—become 'a holy priesthood, to offer up spiritual sacrifices acceptable to God through Jesus Christ' (1 Peter 2:5). Neither is there a special 'clergy' because all 'will be spoken of as ministers of our God.'" [73] **"For I, the L**ORD**, love justice … I will direct their work in truth, and I will make an everlasting covenant with them." 61:8**

Isaiah responds. **I will greatly rejoice in the L**ORD**, my soul shall be joyful in my God; for he has clothed me with garments of salvation, he has covered me with the robe of righteousness. 61:10** Those who have been baptized into Christ have put on Christ, clothed with his righteousness through faith in him. (Galatians 3:26-27).

For Zion's sake I will not hold my peace, and for Jerusalem's sake I will not rest, until the righteousness thereof goes forth as brightness, and the salvation thereof as a lamp that burns. 62:1 The New Jerusalem is the Lamb's bride, "having the glory of God." (Rev. 21:9-11) The church is Christ's wife (Eph. 5:25-32). Righteousness and salvation are to go forth from God's people as a shining bright light as they proclaim the gospel of Christ. Jesus said to his disciples, "Let your light so shine before men, that they may see your good works and glorify your father who is in heaven." (Matthew 5:16) We are to reflect Christ, "the light of the world." (John 8:12)

---

[73] Don Shackelford, Ibid., p. 604

The Gentiles shall see your righteousness ... and you shall be called by a new name, which the mouth of the LORD shall name. 62:2 The new name is "Christian." We read in 1 Peter 4:16, "If anyone suffers as a **Christian**, let him not be ashamed, but let him glorify God in that name." ESV The Gentiles would see God's righteousness before the new name would be given. In Acts 9:15, Christ said concerning Saul (Paul), "He is a chosen vessel unto me, to bear **my name** before the Gentiles." In Acts 10, Cornelius and his household became the **first Gentile converts** to Christ, and the church in Jerusalem "glorified God, saying, 'Then God has also granted to the Gentiles repentance unto life.'" (Acts 11:18) Then Saul joined Barnabas in teaching many in Antioch, a Gentile city. "And the disciples were first **called Christians** in Antioch." (Acts 11:25-26) After the Gentiles saw God's righteousness, the new name "Christian" was given. Those that are in the church of Christ, the bride of Christ, glorify God by calling themselves Christians. A wife should wear her husband's name.

You shall no more be termed Forsaken; neither shall your land any more be termed Desolate: but you shall be called Hephzibah and your land Beulah; for the LORD delights in you, and your land shall be married. 62:4 The new name could not be "Hephzibah" or "Beulah" because neither of these was a new name. They are descriptive in their meaning: *Hephzibah* – "My delight is in her" and *Beulah* – "married." In Isaiah 57:13, the LORD said, "He that puts his trust in me shall possess the land and shall inherit my holy mountain." Zion is God's holy mountain. Christ the Lamb is standing on mount Zion before the throne of God with the redeemed from the earth. (Revelation 14:1-3) This land is called *Beulah – married,* because this is where the marriage of the Lamb takes place. (Rev. 19:5-9) Christ's delight is in his bride, the redeemed.

I have set watchmen upon your walls, O Jerusalem. 62:6 These watchmen are the "apostles, prophets, evangelists, pastors and teachers." (Ephesians 4:11-12)

Build up the highway! Lift up a banner! 62:10 ^{NKJV} Shackelford says, "The **highway** and **a standard** are both evidences of the messianic intent, as they were in chapter 11. Here, we see the messianic kingdom and its influence over the entire world. The highway represents access to the Lord. He would lift up His standard, or sign, and gather His people to Himself from all parts of the earth." [74]

"Say to the daughter of Zion, 'Behold, your salvation comes; behold, his reward is with him.'" 62:11 Hailey observes, "The prophet is looking to that time when the glory of Zion will be complete through the Savior; then the Lord's reward to the people will be a dwelling place in His presence." [75] (cf. 40:10) **And they shall call them The Holy People, The redeemed of the LORD; and you shall be called Sought out, a city not forsaken. 62:12**

Who is this that comes from Edom, with dyed garments from Bozrah? 63:1 Edom aided the Babylonians in the destruction of Jerusalem in 586 BC (Obadiah 11-12); Bozrah was a chief city in Edom. The Edomites represent all who are now seeking to destroy the New Jerusalem. Who is the one whose clothes are stained with blood by defeating the enemies of God's people? Christ answers, **"I who speak in righteousness, mighty to save… For I have trodden the winepress alone … For I have trodden them in My anger and trampled them in My fury; their blood is sprinkled upon My garments, and I have stained all My robes. For the day of vengeance is in My heart, and the year of My redeemed has come." 63:1, 3-4** ^{NKJV} The key word is **alone**.

---

[74] Don Shackelford, Ibid., p. 610
[75] Homer Hailey, *A Commentary on Isaiah*, p. 500

Jesus died **alone** on the cross—forsaken by his disciples (Matthew 26:56) and by God (Matthew 27:46). In conquering Satan, Jesus had to tread the winepress **alone** as he shed his blood. In payment for our sins, it was his blood for our blood. On Judgment Day, the blood of God's enemies will be shed (Rev. 14:19-20). God the Father has "committed all judgment to the Son." (John 5:22) Christ **alone** will slay his enemies with the sword from his mouth when he says to them, "Depart you cursed." He will execute God's wrath upon those who reject his atoning sacrifice. Revelation 19:15 says of Christ, who is described as The Word of God, "He himself treads the winepress of the fierceness and wrath of the Almighty God." On that day, his garments will be stained with the blood of his enemies, as he figuratively treads the winepress of God's wrath. His **own arm brought salvation. 63:5** (cf. 59:16) As in Isaiah 53, salvation is spoken of in the past tense, because of its certainty.

I will mention the loving kindnesses of the LORD and the praises of the LORD, according to all that the LORD has bestowed on us. 63:7 Isaiah calls attention to God's covenant-love. When his chosen people rebelled against him, he punished them with oppressors. But when they repented, he delivered them. Then they would praise him for their salvation and for being faithful to his promises. **In all their affliction, he was afflicted** (Judges 10:16)**, and the Angel of his presence saved them; in his love and in his pity, he redeemed them; and he bore them and carried them all the days of old. 63:9** Christ, who is "the image of God" (2 Cor. 4:4), was with Israel in the wilderness (1 Cor. 10:4), in the conquest of Canaan, and all their days as a nation. Abraham and Jacob were their physical fathers, but the prophet acknowledges the truth, saying, **"You, O LORD, are our Father, our Redeemer; your name is from everlasting." 63:16** NKJV

O LORD, why have you made us to err from your ways, and hardened our heart from your fear? 63:17 God created man with a free will; and man can choose between right and wrong. Hearts are hardened when God reveals himself and his words to men and they refuse to obey him. When they suffer for their sins, they will blame God for their choices. They often will say, "Well, God just made me that way!" Isaiah pleads with God to return to his inheritance for the sake of his faithful servants.

The people of your holiness have possessed it but a little while; our adversaries have trodden down your sanctuary. 63:18 Isaiah is predicting the destruction of the temple in Jerusalem, God's sanctuary, and God's chosen people would feel that they had possessed the temple for only a short time.

We have become like those over whom you have never ruled, like those who are not called by your name. 63:19 ESV As exiles in Babylon, it would seem to them like God had never called them to be his chosen people.

Oh that you would rend the heavens and come down, that the mountains might quake at your presence—and that the nations might tremble at your presence! 64:1, 2 ESV Isaiah is desiring for God to show his great power and presence as he did at Mount Sinai. (Exodus 19:16-20)

For since the beginning of the world men have not heard, nor perceived by the ear, neither has the eye seen ... what he has prepared for him that waits for him. 64:4 The apostle Paul quotes this verse in 1 Corinthians 2:9, as he speaks of the hidden wisdom of God. When the last Day of the Lord comes at the end of time, God will show his power and majesty in an even greater measure than he did at Mount Sinai. "The heavens shall pass away with a great noise, and the elements shall melt with fervent heat, the earth also and the works that are therein shall be burned up" and "all these things shall be dissolved." For those who love God and have waited for him, there will be "new heavens and a new earth, wherein righteousness dwells." (2 Peter 3:10-13)

You meet him that rejoices and works righteousness, those that remember you in your ways. 64:5 Just as the LORD met with Moses, God manifests himself to those who love and obey him. Jesus said, "If a man loves me, he will keep my words; and my Father will love him, and we will come unto him and make our abode with him." (John 14:22-23) In heaven, the faithful servants of God shall see his face. (Rev. 22:4) However, the majority of Israel did not have fellowship with God. **Behold, you are angry; for we have sinned ... We are all as an unclean thing, and all our righteousnesses are as filthy rags." 64:5-6**

But now, O LORD, you are our father; we are the clay, and you are our potter; and all we are the work of your hand. 64:8 Isaiah is appealing to God on behalf of his nation, not upon merits of their righteousness, but upon his relationship to them as their father and creator. **Do not be furious, O LORD, nor remember iniquity forever; indeed, please look—we all are Your people! 64:9** ᴺᴷᴶⱽ The destruction of the cites of Judah, including Jerusalem and the temple, is described in verses 10-11, and then Isaiah asks, **"Will you restrain yourself at these things, O LORD?" 64:12** ᴱˢⱽ Would God fail to act on behalf of his people?

"I am sought of them that asked not for me; I am found of them that sought me not. I said, 'Behold me,

behold me,' unto a nation that was not called by my name." 65:1 God is speaking about the Gentiles, according to Romans 10:12-20. Shackelford says, "The nation of Judah had prayed to God in a time of distress on the basis that they were His people. His reply emphasized that He was rejecting them but would be found by a people who had not sought Him. No longer would they be accepted because of a physical relationship (being the seed of Abraham). In truth, being acceptable to God had never been based on this alone. It had always come through having a faith like that of Abraham (Gal. 3:6-9). The Gentiles would be justified by faith, as was Abraham." [76] These nations will be called through the gospel. (Matt. 28:18-19; Mark 16:15-16)

"I have spread out my hands all the day unto a rebellious people, which walk in a way that was not good, after their own thoughts." 65:2 Paul quotes this verse in Romans 10:21. Throughout most of their history, Israel had rejected God's ways for their own ways. Even during the period of the judges, "every man did that which was right in his own eyes." (Judges 21:25). God tells how they had provoked him with their idolatry and lawlessness while saying, **"I am holier than you!" 65:5**

"I may not destroy them all. I will bring forth a seed out of Jacob, and out of Judah an inheritor of my mountains; and my elect shall inherit it, and my servants shall dwell there." 65:8-9 God will spare a remnant, when he destroys the wicked. Christ is the Seed that would come out of Jacob (Galatians 3:8,14-16). He will come as "a little one" – a baby (9:6) and "a small one" that would become "a strong nation." (60:2) God had promised Abraham, Isaac, and Jacob, "In your seed shall all the nations of the earth be blessed." (Gen. 22:18; 26:4; 28:14)

---

[76] Don Shackelford, Ibid., 629-630

The remnant will be blessed in Christ, who was of the tribe of Judah. They are called "children of God" and "heirs of God, and joint-heirs with Christ" in Romans 8:16-17. Their inheritance is in heaven. (1 Peter 1:3-4)

In **65:10,** God figuratively describes the blessing of those who have sought him. **Sharon** was the fertile plain between Mount Carmel and Joppa. **Achor** was a barren valley between Jericho and Jerusalem. Hosea had said the LORD would give "the valley of Achor for a door of hope." (Hosea 2:15) **Achor** means "trouble." Hope would replace trouble.

"But you who forsake the LORD, who forget my holy mountain, who set a table for Fortune, and who fill cups of wine for Destiny, I will destine you for the sword." 65:11 ᴺᴬˢᴮ **Fortune** and **Destiny** were pagan deities. Today, many are seeking the fortunes of material wealth instead of God; they trust in the destiny promised by the worldly wise. The LORD explains why he will punish the disobedient— **"because, when I called, you did not answer; when I spoke, you did not hear, but did evil before my eyes." 65:12** Sharp contrasts are made in **65:13-14** between the servants of God and the disobedient—blessings for one and sorrows for the other.

The LORD said to unfaithful physical Israel, **"And you shall leave your name for a curse unto my chosen; for the Lord GOD shall slay you and call his servants by another name." 65:15** Physical Israel would cease being God's people. The name "Israel" (power with God) would be given to God's chosen people in Christ. "Christian" will be the other name for God's servants. (Isaiah 62:2; Acts 11:26)

"He who blesses himself in the earth shall bless himself in the God of truth." 65:16 Christ came to "bear witness to the truth." (John 18:37) "Grace and truth came by Jesus Christ." (John 1:17) The new covenant of Christ provides complete forgiveness of sins. "Their sins and iniquities I will remember no more." This promise is made in Jeremiah 31:31-34 and fulfilled in Hebrews 10:14-17.

"For behold, I create new heavens and a new earth; and the former shall not be remembered or come to mind." 65:17 In the beginning, God created the heavens and the earth for man's dwelling place. (Gen.1:1) After the exile in Babylon for 70 years, the Jews had a new home when they were able to return to Jerusalem in 536 BC, a typical fulfillment of Isaiah 65:17. This prophecy is now spiritually fulfilled in the church. But the ultimate fulfillment is heaven, our eternal home. Peter and his fellow Christians were *"a new creation"* (2 Cor. 5:17), having been *"born again"* (1 Peter 1:22), and enjoying *"all things that pertain to life and godliness"* (2 Pet. 1:3); but they still were looking *"for new heavens and a new earth, in which righteousness dwells."* (2 Peter 3:13)

"But be glad and rejoice forever in that which I create; for behold I create Jerusalem a rejoicing, and her people a joy." 65:18 Shackelford says, "The new Jerusalem was to have no **weeping** or **the sound of crying** (v. 19). Premature deaths would be abolished (v. 20), and eviction from homes and fields would be a thing of the past (vv. 21-23). The people and their descendants would be **blessed by the Lord** (v. 23) ... He promised to hear and **answer** the people's call[s] even before they could call ... (v. 24). This reminds us of the description of heaven given by the apostle John (Rev. 21:1-5)." [77]

"The wolf and the lamb shall feed together." 65:25 The peaceable new home in heaven will be free from dangers as symbolized by the wolf and the lamb eating

---

[77] Don Shackelford, Ibid., p. 637

together. This language is similar to that in 11:6, where the peaceable nature of Christ's kingdom is described; **"and dust will be the serpent's meat"** is related to Genesis 3:14, where the serpent is cursed.

Thus says the LORD, "Heaven is My throne, and earth is My footstool. Where then is a house you could build for Me?" 66:1 NASB When King Solomon dedicated the beautiful temple in Jerusalem to God, he acknowledged to the LORD that "the heaven and heaven of heavens cannot contain thee, how much less this house that I have built." (1 Kings 8:27) Shackelford says, "God, the Creator of heaven and earth, cannot be confined in a house built by men. Certainly, God's presence was in the temple, as it is today in the assembly of Christians (1 Cor. 3:16; 6:19, 20). However, God indwells all the heavens and earth." [78] Isaiah had predicted the destruction of Solomon's temple. (63:18) After their exile in Babylon, the Jews would be permitted to return to Jerusalem to rebuild the temple. (Ezra 1:1-3) Jesus and his followers predicted the destruction of this temple. (Matthew 24:1-34; Acts 6:8-14) Stephen gives the reason for this destruction, saying, "The Most High does not dwell in temples made with hands," and then he quotes Isaiah 66:1-2. The temple in Jerusalem was destroyed by the Romans in AD 70.

"But to this one I will look, to him who is humble and contrite of spirit, and who trembles at My word." 66:2 NASB God dwells with the humble person who respects His word. Isaiah had stated in 57:15, "For thus says the high and lofty One that inhabits eternity, whose name is Holy: 'I dwell in the high and holy place with him also that is of a contrite and humble spirit, to revive the spirit of the humble, and to revive the heart of the contrite ones.'"

---

[78] Shackelford, Ibid., p. 641

"But he who kills an ox is like one who slays a man; he who sacrifices a lamb is like the one who breaks a dog's neck; he who offers a grain offering is like one who offers swine's blood; he who burns incense is like one who blesses an idol. As they have chosen their own ways, and their soul delights in their abominations, so I will choose their punishments and I will bring on them what they dread. Because I called, but no one answered; I spoke, but they did not listen. And they did evil in My sight and chose that in which I did not delight." 66:3-4 ^{NASB} If one refuses to listen to God and chooses his own ways, his sacrifices and offerings are offensive to God, and such worship is idolatry, because he is worshiping himself—not the LORD. In contrast, God will dwell with those of contrite and humble hearts that have reverence for His word.

Hear the word of the LORD, you that tremble at his word: "Your brethren who hated you, that cast you out for my name's sake, said, 'Let the LORD be glorified;' but he shall appear to your joy, and they shall be ashamed." 66:5 Jews that would believe in Christ would hated, excluded, and mocked by their Jewish brethren. But these unbelievers would be put to shame.

Hear that uproar from the city, hear the noise from the temple! It is the sound of the LORD repaying his enemies all they deserve. 66:6 ^{NIV} Hailey states, "The entire passage (vv. 1-6) seems to point to the close of the old Jewish order when Jerusalem and the temple were destroyed (A.D. 70)." [79] The LORD would punish these Jewish mockers and persecutors with this destruction.

"Before she was in labor, she gave birth; before her pain came, she delivered a male child." 66:7 ^{NKJV} Before

---

[79] Homer Hailey, Ibid., p. 523

the pain that accompanied the destruction of physical Jerusalem with its temple, spiritual Zion (God's faithful remnant) gave birth to the long-expected Servant, the Messiah, who would "suddenly come to his temple." (Malachi 3:1)

Who has heard such a thing? Who has seen such things? ... Shall a nation be born at once? For as soon as Zion travailed, she brought forth her children. 66:8 Just fifty days after his suffering and death, Christ established the eternal kingdom of God predicted in Daniel 2:44. In one day, the Day of Pentecost, three thousand souls were added to his holy nation (Acts 2); and it grew rapidly. (Acts 4:4; 5:14; 6:7)

"Rejoice with Jerusalem and be glad with her, all you that love her; rejoice for joy with her, all you that mourn for her." 66:10 Those who would mourn over the fall of the old physical Jerusalem could rejoice with the new Jerusalem, the church with her eternal blessings.

"Behold, I will extend peace to her like a river, and the glory of the Gentiles like a flowing stream." 66:12 The LORD would bless his people with a **peace** that surpasses understanding. (Philippians 4:7) The church would grow in great numbers with the conversion of the Gentiles. (Acts 11:18-26) In Isaiah 2:2, the prophet had said that "all nations shall flow unto it." Isaiah begins his prophecies of comfort in 40:1-2 with these words of hope, "Comfort ye, comfort ye my people," says your God. "Speak comfortably to Jerusalem." And he concludes with this promise, **"and you shall be comforted in Jerusalem." 66:13.** Jerusalem is not the literal city but the city of Galatians 4:25-26, Hebrews 12:22, and Revelation 21. God's people will find peace and comfort in the New Jerusalem, the church.

And when you see this, your heart shall rejoice… the hand of the LORD shall be known toward his servants. 66:14 The church began with a demonstration of God's power, and believers were filled with joy and gladness. (Mark 9:1; Acts 2:46; Acts 4:33; Acts 8:39; Acts 9:31; Acts 13:52) The power of God to bless will be fully revealed to the New Jerusalem in heaven.

But the LORD also will make known **his indignation toward his enemies. For behold, the LORD will come with fire. 66:14, 15** Fire symbolizes God's judgment. "The Lord Jesus shall be revealed from heaven with his mighty angels, in flaming fire taking vengeance on those that know not God and that obey not the gospel of our Lord Jesus Christ; who shall be punished with everlasting destruction from the presence of the Lord and from the glory of his power." (2 Thess. 1:7-9) The LORD will judge all flesh, including those that seek to sanctify and purify themselves with their idolatries. (vv. 16, 17)

"I will gather all nations and tongues; and they shall see my glory." 66:18 The purpose of Christ's coming into the world was to bless all nations. Those who escaped Satan's dominion of darkness were sent to evangelize all nations declaring Christ's glory. (**vv.19-21**) The **sign** set among them would be Jesus' resurrection from the dead. (Matt. 12:38-40) Christ's chosen people are "a royal priesthood, a holy nation" to proclaim his praises for calling them "out of darkness into his marvelous light." (1 Peter 2:9).

"For as the new heavens and the new earth, which I will make, shall remain before me," says the LORD, "So shall your seed and your name remain … all flesh shall come to worship before me." 66:22-23 The new heavens and the new earth will remain forever (Rev. 21:1-3), and so shall God's faithful people of all nations remain in God's dwelling place forever worshiping Him. (Rev. 7:9-17)

Isaiah closes with a symbolic description of those in hell who had transgressed against God, saying, **"for their worm shall not die, neither shall their fire be quenched." 66:24** Their judgment is final.

Review Questions on Isaiah 58 – 66

1. God told Isaiah to tell his people their _____.

2. The people were religious but were _____.

3. "But your _____ have separated between you and your God." 59:2

4. "Our transgressions are _____ before you, and our sins _____ against us." 59:12

5. "The _____ shall come to Zion, and to them who _____ _____ transgression in Jacob." 59:20

6. "Arise, _____; for your _____ has come!" 60:1

7. "And the _____ shall come to your light." 60:3

8. "The LORD shall be to you an everlasting _____, and your God your _____." 60:19

9. "The _____ of the Lord GOD is upon me… the LORD has anointed me to preach _____ _____." 61:1

10. _____ read Isaiah 61:1-2 in the synagogue and said, "Today this Scripture has been fulfilled in your hearing."

11. Christ would "give them _____ for ashes." 61:3

12. "I will make an everlasting _____." 61:8

13. "I will greatly rejoice in the Lord… he has covered me with the robe of _____." 61:10

14. "The _____ shall see your righteousness … and you shall be called by a new _____, which the mouth of the LORD shall _____." 62:2

15. "And the disciples were first called _____ in Antioch," which was a _____ city. Acts 11:26

16. Who has "trodden the winepress alone"? 63:3
    _____

17. "We are all as an _____ thing, and all our righteousness acts are as _____ _____." 64:6

18. "I have spread out my hands … unto a _____ people, which walk…after their own _____." 65:2

19. God's people had provoked him with their idolatry while saying, "I am _____ than you!" 65:3-5

20. "I create new _____ and a new _____." 65:17

21. "I create Jerusalem a _____." 65:18

22. In the New Jerusalem, there will be no _____. 65:19

23. Thus says the LORD, "Heaven is My _____, and earth is My_____." 66:1 NKJV

24. "But to this one will I look, to him who is _____ and _____ of spirit, and who _____ at My word." 66:2 NASB

25. Who is the "male-child" of Isaiah 66:7? _____

www.ingramcontent.com/pod-product-compliance
Lightning Source LLC
Chambersburg PA
CBHW060824050426
42453CB00008B/572